UNLIKELY
BROTHERS

ALSO BY JOHN PRENDERGAST

The Enough Moment (with Don Cheadle)

Not On Our Watch (with Don Cheadle)

Blood and Soil

God, Oil, and Country

Crisis Response

Frontline Diplomacy

Crisis and Hope in Africa

Civilian Devastation

Without Troops and Tanks (with Mark Duffield)

Left to right: Michael, David, Elsie, Sabrina, André, Denise, J.P., and Philana

UNLIKELY BROTHERS

Our Story of Adventure, Loss,
and Redemption

JOHN PRENDERGAST

&

MICHAEL MATTOCKS

CROWN PUBLISHERS

New York

Published in the United States by Crown Publishers, an imprint of the Crown Publishing Group, a division of Random House, Inc., New York.
www.crownpublishing.com

CROWN and the Crown colophon are registered trademarks of Random House, Inc.

Library of Congress Cataloging-in-Publication Data

Prendergast, John, 1963–
　　Unlikely Brothers / John Prendergast & Michael Mattocks. —1st ed.
　　　p. cm.
　　1. Prendergast, John, 1963– 2. Mattocks, Michael. 3. Big Brothers of America—Case studies. 4. Friendship—United States—Case studies. 5. Human rights workers—United States—Biography. 6. Drug dealers—United States—Biography. I. Mattocks, Michael. II. Title.

　　HV881.P725 2011
　　323.092'273—dc22
　　[B]　　　　　　　　　　　　　　　　　　　2010042790

ISBN 978-0-307-46484-2
eISBN 978-0-307-46486-6

Printed in the United States of America

Jacket design by K1474@A-MEN PROJECT
Jacket Sam Chung@A-MEN PROJECT
Photograph on page 229 courtesy of Ann Curry, NBC News

10 9 8 7 6 5 4 3 2 1

First Edition

We dedicate this book to our fathers and our brothers,

both the ones who are still here on earth and the ones

that have departed for what we hope are greener pastures.

We are sorry for so many things that happened, and finally

forgive you for the rest.

JOHN AND MICHAEL
WASHINGTON, D.C.

1. "He Ain't Heavy, Father,..."

MICHAEL MATTOCKS

Now, you got to remember I was little when all this started. I know now how fucked up my childhood was, but I didn't know it then. I just lived it—me, my mom and Willie, my little brother James, and my big sister Sabrina. We were living in a big old run-down house in Washington, D.C., with my grandparents, aunts, and uncles piled in on top of us. We all slept in one big room. Back in them days we had enough to eat, but it wasn't like anybody was cooking family meals. We kids would get some cereal if we were hungry. To a little kid, living all together like this was fun. One of the earliest things I remember, though, was my mom and them crying. My aunt Francine's husband beat her to death with an iron, wrapped her body up, stuffed her in the wall where he lived, plastered it over, and painted the wall. I got a cousin who remembers that too. He was small, but he remembers. Aunt Francine was his mother.

My mom has always been a real pretty lady. Not tall, but proud and upright like a queen. Her dad—my grandfather—was real hard on her. With us kids he was okay, but he drank, and he could be mean to my grandmother and to their kids. Not a one of my mother's brothers and sisters—and there were thirteen of them—turned out right. What saved my mom was that she had Willie, her husband, who worked construction and always brought his pay home to look after us. Willie was slim and dark-skinned, with very wide-set eyes and a big smile. Always wore a goofy little corduroy cap. On weekends he would take us kids out to Sandy Point Beach near Annapolis and teach us how to fish, and if we met up with anybody, he'd introduce us as his kids. Willie was a hugging man—always wrapping us kids up in his arms.

For a long time, I thought Willie was my dad—even though he had a different last name. You don't think about that stuff when you're a kid.

Everything changed when my grandfather passed. Grandma sold the house where we all lived together, and everybody went their own way. She could have held the family together—she was the grandmother. She had that power. But her thirteen children were all beefing with each other, so she sold the house, and we all just fell apart. By that time, my mom had had my little brother David and my sister Elsie too, so there were seven of us in our family: five kids, Willie, and my mom.

We moved to an apartment in Landover, Maryland. But we didn't stay there long because one day Willie took me and my little brother James to go see his friend Mr. Morris, and as we were walking up the alley, Willie just fell out. His eyes rolled up and down he went. James and I must have been crying real bad, because Mr. Morris came running out and called the ambulance. I remember the doctors telling my mom that Willie had an aneurysm in his brain and to "expect some changes." Some changes? Willie was gone in the VA hospital six months, and when he came out, he took one look at my mom—mother of his children—and said, "I don't know you." Next day, he took

David with him when he went back to the hospital to pick up some medicine, and he forgot him there. David must have been about three years old. My mom was screaming, "Where is he? Where is my baby?" and Willie kept saying, "I left him here with you." He didn't have any idea. It took my mom forty-nine hours to find little David; some homeless lady had kidnapped him from the hospital and taken him back to the shelter, at Second and D, where she was staying. Luckily, a sharp-eyed social worker there noticed that the woman suddenly had a child who obviously wasn't hers, and the social worker called the police.

Not long after we got David back, Willie drifted off. He didn't know who we were, and he was going to look for his own people. He left my mom with five children.

That must be when we became homeless; I was six. I don't remember how it all went down, but I know there was one shelter after another because they never let you stay in any one for more than a few nights. Sometimes we stayed in these slum-ass motels the city put us in—dirty, cheesy places full of roaches. One time the city put us and about fifty other families in a school at Fourth and O. They pushed the desks aside and set up cots, and we all had to be out of there in the morning before the children showed up.

Most of all I remember carrying our stuff around the streets in Hefty bags, and not knowing in the morning where I'd be sleeping that night.

But here's the thing: Nobody should feel sorry for us, the way we was back then. I know it sounds funny, but we were happy—at least us kids. We didn't know it was bad. My mother cared a lot about us. She made sure we ate every day, even if it was just a little something. If she had a little money, she'd get us a McDonald's even if we had to split a cheeseburger three ways.

I remember us standing at a bus stop one time real hungry, and my mom gathered some change, and all she could get us was a couple of twenty-five-cent cupcakes so that we'd have something in our stomachs. That she tried so hard meant a lot to us. Those hunger pains would never really go away, though. Often we would have canned meat. That shit smelled like dog food out of the can, but my mom somehow made it taste real good.

Our bouncing from shelter to shelter went on for a couple of years. One time my mom took us to her sister, our Aunt Evelyn's house, and asked if could we spend the night, and Aunt Evelyn told my mom no. I don't know why she did that, but like I said, the family kind of came apart after my grandfather passed. Thing is, we never slept on the street. Mom would find us a shelter for a few days, and then we'd be out on the streets again, in the heat, hauling our stuff around in those black Hefty bags.

My mom could have put us in foster care, but she didn't. Around that time, Aunt Evelyn gave up her kids, all seven of them. I don't know where she went, but she was smoking crack, and one day she just walked out on her kids, right out of the house they owned off Florida Avenue. Mom was there that day, visiting, and she just rounded up Aunt Evelyn's kids and brought them to the shelter and hid them in our room there. They was our cousins, our family, and we just all crammed in together and didn't think twice about it.

Mom saw what happened to Aunt Evelyn, and she kept us all together. So for a little while, she was raising all of us and five of Aunt Evelyn's kids right there in the shelter. The two eldest cut out once their mom left them, and later on, two of them stuck around and lived with us. Mom didn't know much about raising children, but she knew enough not to let us go. I remember we were at a shelter place, and some people came to my mom and said they wanted to take us. Man, mom flipped out. "You ain't taking my motherfucking kids!" Screaming and throwing shit—she really went off. There wasn't anything wrong with us as a family, really; we just didn't have money, plain and simple. We also didn't get a whole lot of hugging once Willie was gone. Mom was all about just getting us through the day—ten-hut, pick up your things there, look after your little brother, find your other shoe. Just getting her own five kids up and fed and off to the next shelter was about all she could do.

Pretty soon, it was time for me and James and Sabrina to go to school. There'd be a van come take us to Thompson Elementary, pick us up at whatever shelter and take us back there. No one knew we was from the shelter because we hid it real good. My sister Sabrina was seven, one year older than me; she was more like the big brother than a big sister. She was a little bitty thing—pretty like my mom—but man, you didn't want to fuck with Sabrina. A kid would tease us about our raggedy-ass no-name-brand shoes, and Sabrina would come down on him like a hurricane. Always ready to throw the fuck down, and it wouldn't matter how big the other kid was. Always getting in trouble for fighting and wouldn't give a fuck. To her, it didn't matter going to the principal's office. She had her little brothers to defend. Like a mama bear with her cubs; that was Sabrina. To this day, I've never seen her lose a fight.

James, he was one year younger than me, and he was Willie's boy for sure because they had the same last name: Whitaker. James was small and skinny, and darker than me. We have Cherokee in our blood from way back, and you could really see it in James. We were tight, being the two big boys of the family. We did everything together. But he and Sabrina shared something that I never did—that love of fighting. James could be going along just fine and then something would set him off. Even as a little kid I remember being shocked by it. We'd be out playing in the street with some kids and I'd think everything was fine, and suddenly James would be throwing his fists on some kid like to kill him.

I can't be sure why James was like that, but part of it maybe was because he and Willie had a special bond, more than Sabrina or me. It hurt us all when Willie left, that's for sure, but it hurt James the most. He was in a lotta pain for a long time from that. And he was real angry at my mom over it, but I didn't know why. He turned that anger on other people, and most times I wouldn't even see it coming. That's where I think his love of fighting came from. James, he never did get over Willie leaving.

I wasn't like that. I didn't really like to fight. I wouldn't get mad like that. It made me feel safe, though, having Sabrina on one side of me and James on the other. Even as little kids, ain't nobody wanted to fuck with either of them, or with me.

JOHN PRENDERGAST

When people learned that I was a big brother to Michael and James, they would always say something about how generous or noble I was. I guess that's one way to look at it, but it sure isn't the whole story. Not even close.

When I first met Michael and James, I was a curious, driven, and emotionally wounded twenty-year-old. At the time, I was talking my way through summer courses at George Washington University, having already attended three other universities, and I was working at the Robert Kennedy Memorial's Youth Policy Institute in some kind of glorified internship. I was on a mission to change the way America addressed the needs of kids living in poverty, to help shine a light on what was called back then the "underclass," and to create an education-to-employment system that would give kids from disadvantaged neighborhoods real equal opportunity. You know, the kind of grandiose dreams a twenty-year-old should have. So becoming a big brother to Michael and James fit right into that, I suppose. But to understand what really propelled me into the lives of these little guys—to gauge the parameters of the hole in my heart that I tried to fill with Michael and James—you have to go back to my own beginnings.

As with all boys, it starts with my father, a Purple Heart awardee nicknamed Jack, who was a giant of a man. He'd studied to be a priest, and though he had veered from that path, he retained an intense and old guard Catholic faith. His personal form of devotion ran the gamut from volunteering at Mother Teresa's soup kitchens and homeless shelters to lying prostrate in front of family planning clinics to protest abortions and going to jail for it regularly.

Here's the kind of man he was: Once a week, when we lived near Philly, Dad visited the sisters of the Regina Mundi Priory, a contemplative order of nuns with physical disabilities, and he took them in two or three shifts in his car to a swimming pool to give them an outing. One of the nuns, though, never went near the water; she sat alone in her wheelchair ten feet away from the pool, locked in a deathly terror of drowning and intense shame about her condition. Each week, Dad knelt before this sweet woman, needling her playfully and gently trying to cajole her into the pool. It took months, but finally she relented. He removed her leg braces, picked her up in his arms—Dad was a rugby and hockey player—and carried her tenderly into the water, holding her until she stopped trembling. Within a few weeks, she was able to float on her own. A couple decades later, I went to visit some of the surviving nuns, who had moved to another convent in New England. That's how I learned about this story. She told me no one in her entire life had ever been as patient and gentle with her as my dad was during that time.

These are the kinds of stories I grew up with. I was constantly being told what a wonderful man my father was.

And for the first seven or eight years of my life, that's how I experienced him. Dad was an old-school traveling salesman for a company called Fred's Frozen Foods. He was a grandmaster at it in the way born salesmen are, and he always knew the angles to approach people. He had an Irishman's bottomless well of funny stories to tell, to soften up the client, and he also had a charismatic but mischievous way of interacting that made everybody around him feel important and at ease. He would walk down the street flashing a big grin and playing tricks on or saying hello to countless passers-by. He loved to draw people out and connect to them. He was a chameleon, a comedian, a people-pleasing tornado of a man.

Dad spent his days on the road with his partner-in-culinary-crime, Uncle Dave Wells, driving a station wagon around to schools and hospitals all over the Midwest, armed with a big dry-ice cooler and deep fryer in back filled with corn dogs, pizza burgers, and breaded pork tenderloins, the kind of gluttonous product line that would make a nutritionist go on a hunger strike in protest.

We always lived in comfortable houses big enough that my younger brother Luke and I had our own rooms. We mostly saw Dad on weekends, but when he was home, he was fully present. One time, for my science fair project Dad and I decided to figure out where a steak comes from. So we went to a prototypical Midwestern cattle ranch, and then we went to the Kansas City stockyards. The whole time, Dad would interview the cows about their impending fate. He'd have full-blown conversations with cows! I mean, the guy was mesmerizingly original and creative. I don't know who was more startled by his tactics, the ranchers or the cows or me, but darned if I didn't win first prize at that science fair with our big, blustery poster boards showing the remarkable transformation from a cow in the field to a steak on a plate, from the cow's point of view.

Dad used his extraordinary storyteller's gift on the neighborhood kids, but especially on Luke and me. We'd both get into one bed at night, and Dad would sit there in the dark with us, spinning out his own versions of *Call of the Wild*, *Tom Sawyer*, and *Adventures of Huckleberry Finn*. He'd start with the skeleton of the original tale and then go off on long, imaginative riffs. I never knew where the real stories ended and Dad's flights of fancy began until later when I read the originals, but I loved Dad's versions. It was never hard getting Luke and me to go to bed when Dad was around. And the stories of his adventures on the road with Uncle Dave! To a kid, they were magical. Who needed television when you had a dad like mine!

When he was on the road, he'd write us stories on postcards, hotel stationery, and airline vomit bags, wherever he could put pen to paper. There was one long-running story he concocted about a family of Native American totem poles who were also secret heroes. We'd seen them at a roadside exhibit in Texas one time when we were bombing around in the station wagon on one of our road trip adventures, and they took on a life of their own through Dad's electrifying tales.

Uncle Dave and Dad were always mixing it up. Once they found themselves in Las Vegas in the same hotel where Elvis Presley was staying. So they got to know a couple of the waiters and either convinced or bribed them to be allowed to bring Elvis his room service meal. They hung around with the King in his hotel suite for a long time shooting the breeze. Another time they were in a big hotel and, in one of their more questionable moments, they found a wheelchair in a storage closet. So Dad got in the chair and Uncle Dave wheeled him into the restaurant, which was full of people at dinnertime. Uncle Dave ran the wheelchair into someone's table and flipped the chair so Dad tumbled out. The diners were horrified, and a few rushed to Dad's help. Suddenly Dad leapt up and shouted, "I'm cured, I'm cured. My god, it's a miracle!!" And the place went nuts. I could go on all day recounting the stories we heard.

And we also saw for ourselves Dad in action. In a Pittsburgh gym and swimming pool Dad used to sneak us into through a little-used basement entrance, he wriggled a meeting for us with Fred Rogers, who had just finished his swim and was just like he was on television in *Mister Rogers' Neighborhood*. In Louisville we met the real Colonel Sanders, resplendent in his white suit, who told us the incredible story of how he started Kentucky Fried Chicken. He told Dad that he had heard of Fred's Frozen Foods and liked what he saw, or tasted, from one breading guy to another, I guess. Dad was beaming the rest of the day, getting the Colonel's stamp of approval like that.

We got to go with Dad to these extraordinary events called "food shows," where restaurateurs and food brokers of all kinds would display their wares in some big auditorium. Luke and I would slide down row after row, sampling these culinary delights and meeting some of the greatest traveling salesmen who ever lived. They were larger-than-life figures, with big laughs, strong handshakes, and endless stories.

And Dad was the biggest of all of them in my eyes.

It was with the neighborhood kids, though, that my dad's goodness really shone. Some of my earliest memories are of Dad driving through the neighborhoods we lived in, rounding up kids to play baseball or football in the park. People called him the Pied Piper; every kid followed him. He was tall and strong, and he had a full head of silver hair from the time he was in his mid-thirties. His smile was as wide as a piano keyboard; people couldn't help but like him. If we were driving along and saw an old lady who had to cross the road, Dad would stop the car right in the intersection and make us kids get out with him, and then we'd help the old lady cross the street, with the cars behind us honking away.

Dad would pitch or quarterback for both teams, and he'd keep those kids entertained for hours with jokes, pratfalls, and high-energy goofballism. And if one of the kids clowned with him—pirouetting on his way to second base, crossing the end zone in a back flip—Dad would laugh and flatter him by performing his own deft imitation. I wish I could have frozen time right there . . .

A big shadow hung over my childhood, though, amidst all this sunshine: We moved from city to city every few years. We left Indianapolis for Kansas City when I was in kindergarten, and we moved from Kansas City to Fort Wayne several years later, and then we went on to Philadelphia. In between, we would land for memorable stints in Dad's hometown of Pittsburgh, as well as the farms of my mom's people in Kansas and Oklahoma. Dad fit in every place we went; he was the most popular grownup among the kids for miles around. It was not unusual for a knock on the door to come at any time, and a kid there to ask, "Can Mr. P come out and play?"

But moving really took its emotional toll on me. It always seemed that the minute I was starting to draw whole breaths in a new place, we'd be on to the next. Each time, a little reservoir of sadness and self-doubt, isolation and anger, collected inside me because once again I'd be the outsider, the loner kid on the playground. Admittedly, I was a sensitive kid. But the regular moving crushed my spirit in ways that I had increasing trouble recovering from. The day the moving van showed up in Kansas City, I drew a few pitchers of water from the kitchen sink, carefully carried them outside, and poured them into the soil beneath the hedges to make a vast arsenal of mud. I peppered the side of that van with the mud, trying to erase the moving company's name, Bekins. I caught hell and a half for that; the Bekins driver nearly pulled my arm out of its socket.

And then, somewhere around the time I was eight, an eerie darkness began falling across my relationship with Dad. I'm sure I was full of unspoken resentment toward him for uprooting us every few years. What I felt coming from Dad, though, was a new and growing impatience and anger with me that I couldn't figure out. For example, I remember following Dad and all the neighborhood kids up to the park one day for a big baseball game. Everybody was clowning around—tripping each other on the grass, running the bases backward—and Dad was laughing, . . . until I got into the spirit and came to bat with my mitt on my head. Suddenly it was though a cloud had rolled in front of the sun. "Goddammit, J.P.!" he barked, and I shrank down into my shoes. On the way home after he dropped the other kids off, he started yelling at me for another perceived offense, and when I talked back to him, he spit at me in the backseat where I was sitting right next to Luke, and then he kicked me out of the car, making me walk the rest of the way home.

Again and again, it seemed, Dad would single me out for a harsh, relentless, and unexpected scolding—often when I felt I was doing nothing wrong. The forcefulness of the anger was shocking and profoundly destabilizing to me, and so contrary to his sunny persona. He would pay so much positive attention to strangers, and then turn on me like a wolf. Once I got stung by a bee and he screamed at me for not spraying myself with insect repellent. He went on and on, his face bright red with fury at my mistake, all the while my hand swelling up because of my extreme allergy to insect bites. He was viscerally, blindly affected by my mistakes, or by any hint of defiance.

Luke, Dad, and J.P.

Most importantly, I think, he wanted me to be perfect—a standard I could never meet no matter how hard I tried. The weight of his expectations was crushing.

When Dad would go off on his sales trips Monday through Friday, Mom was left behind with Luke and me. Mom had coincidentally studied to be a nun while Dad studied for the priesthood before they left their vocations separately, later met, and eventually married each other. She had endless energy for the church, for volunteering to teach art to kids in the Head Start program, for praying in front of family planning clinics (but not going with my dad to get arrested), for supporting the nuns of Mother Teresa's religious order, and for her two boys whom she loved so much and so well. But it was tough for her to have to raise two growing sons while her husband was perpetually on the road and needing to move every few years. Not that Luke and I were bad kids; in fact, just the opposite. We were boys, sure, and we would get into fairly typical trivial scrapes and mischievous mishaps. But we were good student-athletes who didn't break any major laws and didn't come home in drunken stupors.

In fairness, however, we were a handful for my mom, and, in retrospect, I figure there is no way she wasn't a bit subconsciously resentful toward Dad for being away so much. It must have been very difficult for her to be perpetually in his huge shadow, watching him constantly playing the role of the class clown. So by the time he got home from one of his weeklong trips, she'd have assembled a multi-count indictment of every one of Luke's and my transgressions. Taken individually, these wouldn't have caused much of a blink, but remember, this was the pre-cell phone era, which meant that there was a week's worth of inequities for two rambunctious boys, and the litany was bracing for any semi-absent parent. Here I'd be eager for Dad to get home to play and tell his stories, but then, the minute he walked through the door—his pork tenderloin sample cases still in his hands and his overcoat buttoned—Mom would unload: "They clipped all the flowers from the hedges." "They broke the basement window." "They made a mess of the garage." Dad—tired from the road and most likely filled with his own frustrations—would simply snap. He had a legendary Irish temper, and he probably just wanted a drink, and a little peace and quiet. But his rage would all come raining down on me, the eldest son. The man could go from zero to sixty in a heartbeat—face bright red, screaming his head off at me, occasionally with a hint of real blackout violence, and bringing out his belt, which we nicknamed the "whistling wasp." His rage-aholism, usually connected with his drinking, was utterly terrifying. My hero would turn into a monster right before my eyes, and over time his short, frequent, explosive outbursts were devastating.

In each house we moved to, I would have a hiding place to which I would run during these outbursts. In our Kansas City house, the upstairs bathroom had a foldout cabinet that, when opened, would block the door, and to get away from any one of Dad's memorable tirades, I'd run in there, open the drawer, then climb out the window and down off the roof. There was a spot, on the back roof of the garage and underneath a gigantic tree, that was my secret hideout; nobody knew about it, and nobody knew I was up there. I'd sit in there for hours with my hands squeezed against my pounding temples, absolutely invisible to the world, wondering, in my childish, guilt-ridden Catholic way: What did I do wrong? Why can't I be good?

It was in moments like these that my journey toward Michael began.

Back then I didn't forge a tight bond with Luke, who is a year and a half younger than I am. I kept Luke outside the walls. As anyone's little brother would, he tried to follow me around, and I invariably stiff-armed him. Maybe I resented that I took the brunt of my dad's anger and frustration. Dad was so easygoing with Luke, who had a knack for just going along while I couldn't accept a shred of hypocrisy, unfairness, or authoritarianism from my father. Maybe I was jealous of how cool Luke was through thick and thin, while I was so sensitive, volatile, affected, and reactive. I slowly grew such a hard shell around my heart, to protect myself from Dad's anger and the constant moves from city to city, that on some subconscious level I probably feared opening it up a crack to let Luke in. Who knows what else would have rushed in, or rushed out? It was safer for me to build my own little solitary citadel. Luke learned early on not to count on me too much for friendship, and he went his own way.

Even though we weren't as close as we could have been back then, my protective instincts for Luke were already in full incubation, which when combined with my own volatility didn't bode well for anyone who wanted to give Luke a hard time. One time on the school bus in Indiana, some older kid stuck his foot out and tripped Luke when he was walking to the back of the bus. What a mistake. It took a few of the other kids and the bus driver to pull me off the kid who did it, after I set upon him like a wild hyena. Another time I was in the garage and some kid rode up on his bike and said something derogatory to Luke. I came sprinting out of the garage so fast that I almost caught the kid as he sped away on his brand-new ten-speed bike. I didn't see that kid on our block for weeks after that.

As part of his Catholic faith and love of kids, my dad gave money to Boys' Town, the center originally set up for homeless boys that Father Edward Flanagan founded near Omaha in 1917.

An icon from Boys' Town that my father gave me hovers over the memories of my childhood. It was a wallet-sized picture of a smiling boy carrying a smaller, sleeping boy on his back. Beneath them is the legend "He ain't heavy, Father, . . . he's my brother!"

I used to stare at that picture; something about it captivated me. Though I was the big brother in the Prendergast family, it was the little guy I identified with. I wished for somebody like that big brother, somebody to stand up for me and protect me from the irrationality of my father's fury, and from the loneliness that lingered with me wherever we moved to next.

What I think happened later inside my head was a kind of mental and spiritual backflip where I said to myself, okay, if I can't be the little guy, I'll be the big guy. Let me look for someone who doesn't have that protector, because, as I know firsthand, it is the loneliest feeling in the world.

In Fort Wayne I became a teenager, with all that that entails. My relationship with Dad continued to deteriorate, and I never really understood why. I'd try to be good—I brought home nothing but A's, I played on five different sports teams, and never drank or did any drugs. But nothing seemed to invite his approval. To the rest of the world, he was Uncle Jack—the back-slapping, handshake-buzzer-wielding, fart-cushion-planting clown he always was. To kids in the neighborhood, he was an ice-cream truck on a summer day. As I got older, it was as though God had given him only so much goodness to spend, and he doled it out in every direction but mine.

As communication became more difficult, my dad reverted more and more to the Korean War sergeant he had been when he was in his twenties. We were both dug in pretty deep by this time, so when he'd issue an order and I inevitably wouldn't obey, things would escalate quickly, not unlike the worst caricature of a boot camp drill sergeant and the delinquent and defiant draftee. I refused to conform to the buck private to which he had tried to reduce me. He retreated more and more into military mode, and the war was on. Funny thing is, if he'd just have asked me, I would have done anything for him.

Our relationship squeezed down tighter and tighter, to the point where not only did I stop speaking to him but I completely refused to acknowledge his existence. I would look in every direction but his. I would address my mother and brother around the vacuum that I made of my father. At meals, I wouldn't talk at all; if I wanted the salt, I'd catch Luke's eye and slide my eyes toward the salt shaker. Nothing more. Naturally, my anti-theatrics placed a heavier burden on Luke, but that didn't occur to me at all at the time.

Of course, ignoring Dad only enraged him further. I wasn't a little kid anymore. I was getting bigger and bigger. I was an older boy growing into a young man, and I was challenging his authority on his own turf. I was growing physically and intellectually, but basically thumbing my nose at him routinely right in his own house. Now, as an adult, I can see how incredibly painful that must have been for him, especially since he was so poorly equipped to cope with it, or even acknowledge it. It's not like his life experience—raised by a Pittsburgh steelworker, schooled in the Vatican's brand of unquestioning obedience, and then thrust into the cheerful conformity of corporate sales—had given him skills for empathy or introspection. All he saw in me was rebellion, and rudeness. He'd close in on me screaming, especially when he'd had a few drinks, and I'd simply turn into a corner with my head bowed, the emotional equivalent of Muhammad Ali's old rope-a-dope, coldly willing him away as he railed and raged and pushed at my back.

But then, of course, I would turn it all on myself. My new hiding place in Fort Wayne, Indiana, was the neighbors' garage. I'd spend hours crouched beside their rarely used car, my back against the tire, face in my hands, wondering why I was so unlovable.

At just this moment—as if to physically confirm my unlovability—my face exploded with a case of cystic acne for the record books. Knobby red lesions—shiny, greasy, and nauseating—so disfigured my face and neck that Luke took to calling me "The Lizard." As a teenager, I simply squelched any newfound interest in the opposite sex. I kept myself hidden as much as possible behind long hair and a turned-down face. I took refuge in homework and basketball—especially basketball. It was an all-male world in which appearances mattered less than skill or effort, except for when the occasional impolitic kid could be overheard asking, "What's wrong with that guy's face?" I'd inherited my father's natural athleticism and worked at it like a fiend. Neither rain, nor sleet, nor gloom of night would keep me from my appointed hoop rounds. For me, every game—no matter how informal—was Game 7 of the NBA Finals. And I followed professional ball with the concentration of a Zen master, studying Pistol Pete Maravich's arsenal of moves, losing myself in the bottomless minutiae of strategy and statistics. I lofted myself on a cloud of inflated and delusional dreams of someday playing professional basketball.

What so tortured me, at my core, was not just my father's screaming and my acne-ruined face, but the terrible *unfairness* that lay at the heart of it. I was a good kid, and yet all that my father saw were my mistakes and shortcomings, and all the world saw was a mutant lizard. I'd work hard to make friends, and then suddenly we'd be moving to another strange city. It was, to my proto-adolescent self, so massively *unfair*. That word—*unfair*—was etched on a giant boulder at the center of my consciousness; I've spent just about every minute of my life since then trying to scrape it away, in all kinds of rational and irrational ways.

It was this sense of unavenged injustice, I suppose, that led me to my other great passion at the time: superhero comic books. Something about these magical figures overcoming human failings to strike down unfairness resonated deep inside me. The ones I especially liked were the flawed heroes, the guys like Tony Stark in *Iron Man* who drank too much and pushed away everybody who tried to love him, and then exploded out of himself to become an avenger of nearly limitless power. All the best superhero stories seemed to turn on the same plot twist: That moment when a somewhat tormented, loner of a guy like me would undergo a freak accident—being bitten by a radioactive spider, say—and be transformed into a kind of savior or demigod. It's what kept me going, the fantasy that someone as flawed and unlovable as I would suddenly, and unexpectedly, be magically transformed into something else.

Never happened.

Instead, in the summer between eighth grade and freshman year of high school, my mother told me that we were moving again—this time to Philadelphia. It was too much; I cracked up. I fell into long fits of inconsolable staring, punctuated by occasional tears: "I can't do this again. I'm just starting to fit in here a little bit. Don't make me carry this ruined face into an entirely new school!" I descended further into a silent and lonely despair, a thoroughly broken kid.

The only way my parents could coax me into the car for the move to Philadelphia was to agree to the one condition I set upon the transition: that I could attend the same high school Wilt Chamberlain had attended so I could continue pursuing my NBA fantasy. Sure, my parents said. Just get in the car. Of course, once we arrived and they discovered that Wilt's old school was one of the lowest performing in Philadelphia, I was off to Devon Prep, a predominately white Catholic high school run by hard-core, old-school, Hungarian Piarist priests. One of my last memories of that place is being forced to go to a school dance when my basketball team was on a road trip and finding the darkest corner of the gym where I could hide my pock-marked face.

Our new house was in Berwyn, about thirty minutes from downtown Philly. It had four bedrooms, a pool out back, and plenty of trees, and my isolation was absolute. I spent all my time working at various odd jobs, studying, and playing basketball. But while at home at night, I simply hid out in the basement, avoiding my parents, avoiding Luke, avoiding other kids, obsessively making tapes with a cassette recorder and a microphone poised precariously on a sock, mostly of rock bands from the 1960s and early 1970s, an era of peace activism about which I was enthralled. On the tapes, the house's furnace cycling on and off is clearly audible behind the sounds of Led Zeppelin and Jimi Hendrix.

Hard as the move to Philly was, though, it was there that I began to figure out how to confront the unfairness of the world that so confounded me, and my path, ultimately, to Michael began to emerge more clearly.

I was able to talk my way out of Devon Prep and into the much cheaper Archbishop Carroll High School, run by the Christian Brothers order, on the grounds that since I was obviously headed for the NBA, I needed a high school with a bigger basketball program. Carroll wasn't like some of the other Catholic schools. It had no specific uniforms, though a tie was required. And while it didn't officially teach a Dorothy Day kind of activist Catholicism, we did hear a lot, informally, about farmworker organizer Cesar Chavez, peace activist Philip Berrigan, and other figures who stood up against unfairness in the way that Jesus did when he overturned the tables of the moneychangers and merchants who were ripping people off in the temple. What I also found at Archbishop Carroll were three teachers who changed the course of my life.

The first one, Garrett Woznicki, was an indefatigable hippie with thinning long hair and a Jesus beard. Mr. Woz was very unconventional and excitable, jumping around like a talk show host or sitting back with his feet on the desk, cracking wise but breaking down literature like there was no tomorrow. He used to swear a lot in class, and that would get us all going. Some of his analytical insights, though, were like bombs dropping on your head. My brother Luke was also his student, and he once asked Mr. Woz a question about *Catcher in the Rye* and Holden's messianic complex. Mr. Woz wrote out an answer and gave it to Luke. It was so compelling that my brother still has that piece of loose-leaf today.

Mr. Woz not only put before me volumes of Kerouac, Joyce, Sartre, Kierkegaard, and Beckett, but he invited me to think and talk about them. Me! The Lizard! I'd never had anybody so highly value the contents of my skull. He turned reading, for me, into an aerobic sport; I remember devouring books with such ravenous intensity that I would sweat over the pages, my head filled with tales of courage, inquiry, adventure, destiny, and redemption.

serve the people marginalized in our society. The light
though dim, was getting stronger. For the first time I
to get a sense of what I might do with my life. A mission
oming into focus.

he next year I took an evening class at Archbishop Car-
fter basketball practice, and what set it apart was that un-
my gender-segregated daytime classes, there were girls in it.
face was so hideous with acne cysts that I would come in
basketball practice with a towel around my neck or over
head like a monk's hood—to dry my hair, I'd say, but really I
hiding. The teacher—the second great influence of my high
nool career—was Joe Stoutzenberger, another man so lanky it
akes me wonder if the school system paid these guys enough
eat properly. He taught world religion in a way the original
rchbishop Carroll himself probably couldn't have envisioned.
Mr. Stoutz was very Buddhist in his outlook and mannerisms,
and he spent weeks, while standing under the full-color cruci-
fix on the wall, enlightening us on the tenets of other religions
around the world and the centrality of compassion.

Mr. Stoutz led great discussions, and it was in his class that
I finally discovered I had something to offer the world: I could
listen and empathize. I could hear what people were saying,
synthesize their thoughts, and lead discussions in a productive
direction. I was probably particularly motivated because there
were girls in the room, but I wasn't really angling for them. The
acne had made me a virtually asexual being. I only realized later
that my facial and family afflictions had led me to deeper emotional frequencies that helped identify with others' suffering and
pain, which helped me to connect to people much more easily,
especially those who themselves felt isolated. People told me that
they felt "safe" around me, that I was emotionally trustworthy.

One afternoon, I was shooting hoops in the driveway with
Bobby Kennedy, a classmate who had as complex a father relationship as I did. We often spent long hours together processing
the warped and painful father-son dynamic, trying to figure out
what it all meant. That afternoon, Bobby and I were playing
one-on-one and talking when Bobby suddenly said, "Let's get
out of here."

I thought he meant take the train into downtown Philly.
"No," he said, "let's go to New York."

New York? New York was way outside the Berwyn orbit.
"When?" I asked.
"Right now."

Instantly, the idea made perfect sense. Just go. Get away
from Dad, get away from school, get away from the whole world
that judged me by my acne—just flee. Neither of us wanted to
tell our parents what we were about to do, which I guess techni-
cally qualified us as running away. We left the basketball lying
in the driveway. Next thing we knew, we were grabbing onto a
slow-moving Conrail train and hopping on the back as it pulled
out of the station, and we were off to New York.

New York was electrifying and terrifying at the same time for
a couple of fifteen-year-old boys. We didn't want to get rolled the
minute we got off the train, so we practiced looking like New
Yorkers. We stood in Penn Station watching people go by, and
then practicing for each other how New Yorkers walked—with
arms swinging and head held down as though getting ready to
butt people out of the way. Predictably, a couple of Unification-
ists (or as we called them in our youth, "Moonies," a term that
has since then come to be considered derogatory)—who were
all over the place back then and, little did we know, exquisitely

skilled at trolling for lost youth—swooped in on us and with maximum warmth and cheerfulness offered us a place to stay. Not knowing any better, Bobby and I followed them to a hotel that was serving as their New York headquarters. Something made me stop, though. The vibe didn't feel right, and I convinced Bobby to back away with me. The two who had lured us from Penn Station were stricken; they probably thought that if they had gotten us inside, they'd have us for good. They followed us for blocks, trying to get us to go back with them.

Bobby and I had very little money in our pockets, so we went to the YMCA. I went in first, and they gave me one little room that looked like something from a pre-war hospital, with one narrow cot. Bobby and I slept head to toe. Since the rooms were supposed to be for one person, one of us would have to go up to the room, open the window, and drop the key down into the alley so the other could come up as if going to a different room. During the day, we just wandered around, taking it all in. We probably looked like Dustin Hoffman and Jon Voigt from *Midnight Cowboy*. We were unkempt and disheveled, and what's more, I had cut my toe on some glass and was limping around like Hoffman's Ratso Rizzo. Times Square of the late 1970s was a revelation for me. I'd never seen so much homelessness, so many vagrants, so much raw need. I would talk with everyone, learning their stories, trying to understand how they got where they got. The more I saw, the more I wanted to see; I kept pushing Bobby and me toward the seediest parts of town.

After about a week, our money ran out completely, and we went to Covenant House, the famous mission to runaway and homeless children. The people there took us in like long-lost family; after all, their first concern is to make runaways feel safe. They gave us a pretty nice room with a bathroom and let

me soak and bandage my toe. Bob
there. Meanwhile, our parents were
running the shelter must have slowly
flimsy story in passing conversations.
staff, about ten years older than we wer
"Where you boys from?"

We were ready for him, we thought.

"Flatbush," I said.

"Brooklyn," Bobby said at the same ti

The guy smiled. "Which is it?"

"Flatbush."

"Flatbush, yeah."

"So, not Brooklyn," he asked us.

"No sir," Bobby said. "Flatbush."

"Boys," the man said. "Flatbush is *in* Brook
I looked at each other in horror. That hadn't tak

"You guys are from Philadelphia, aren't you
from some pretty disturbed parents who suspect
be here. We aren't throwing you out, but it sure sou
want you to come home."

We were on the train home that afternoon, an
York adventure was over. But the trip—hanging ar
enant House, wandering New York's back alleys—rea
thinking about inequality as it relates to race, addiction,
and homelessness. Those left behind and forgotten in c
New York and Philly seemed particularly badly served
society. The government had a whole Scrabble set full o
nyms for dealing with the poor—AFDC, SSI, HUD, ar
on—yet it seemed that poor people only became poorer
more numerous. Something was wrong. Something was m
ing. The whole situation was *unfair*. There had to be a bet

That I was, in a way, the older boy from the Boys' Town poster. It didn't lift me out of my dark hole, but perhaps a tiny crack in all that blackness had appeared, and a little bit of light was seeping through, illuminating the beginning of a path.

Mr. Stoutz was very big on the notion that having faith in the community is the first step toward serving the community. We read *Siddhartha*, about the Buddha leaving the palace and discovering real life, and Mr. Stoutz made that a requirement of his class—that we leave the palace of suburban Philadelphia and discover other realities. So I began wandering into downtown Philadelphia on the train, sometimes with my best buddy Joe DiStefano, to volunteer at a homeless shelter for men—my first, inchoate attempt to assuage my anguish over injustice by actually doing something about it. I'd go after school or on weekends and do menial jobs—ladling soup, cleaning up—and talk to the guys who'd ended up there. Many of them had spent their lives battling alcohol or drug addiction, and all manner of mental illness, and some, by their accounts, had just had crushingly bad breaks in life.

The people running the shelter warned me not to get too personally invested in the residents; they came and went, and I wouldn't be any good to the organization if I had an emotional stake in any of them. But their pain latched on to me, at the cellular level, like a virus. In retrospect, it may not have been the best thing for my mental health at the time, because each of those gentlemen had his own tale of woe, and little by little I filled myself up with these tales of personal misery, adding them to my own. My acne was really aflame in those days. It was so bad—physically painful, not just emotionally gruesome—that my mother found some charlatan with a suction machine in his office that sucked the lesions off my back and chest with a loud *thunk*, pulling divots of flesh with them and leaving scars that were still with me two decades later.

Meanwhile, the more I ignored and defied my father, the angrier he grew; some evenings ended with him stalking me out of the kitchen through the porch out into the driveway under the basketball hoop and down all the way to the street, screaming at my back, making me feel like a worthless loser. Me. The student-athlete who simultaneously held down a paper route, a lawn-cutting business, and a YMCA gym job, while still volunteering at the homeless shelter. How could he look at me with such anger? And while we're at it, how could there be a God with so much injustice in the world, allowing so much suffering? The leap of great unfairness from the personal to the global was in full development mode.

One night, waiting for the train home to Berwyn from Philadelphia, I stood at the edge of the platform, tortured by the hideous unfairness of everything I was feeling so palpably, strongly considering whether to step in front of the train. The engineer must have seen something was amiss; he blasted his horn uncharacteristically as he pulled into the station. I don't even remember how, or why—maybe I was clinging to that sliver of light I'd discovered in Mr. Stoutz' class—but I stepped back out of the way at the last second.

Meanwhile, my hoop dreams, or rather hoop delusions, were disappearing in a haze of painful injuries. Every year some part of my anatomy failed me. In seventh and eighth grades, the tendonitis was so bad in my wrists that I would tearfully run scalding water on them before games in the vain hope that the cysts would loosen up. My freshman and sophomore seasons were hindered by bone spurs and plantar fasciitis, making every step feel like hypodermic needles were being inserted into my heels. My junior year my cousin landed on my arm and broke it while I was roughhousing in Pittsburgh right before the season, making me miss the entire season. My coach didn't speak to me for weeks after that. And finally my senior year I couldn't run or jump because of tendonitis in my knees. Fed up, Coach Kirsch cut me, but I went to him in tears and begged him to let me stay on the team—I wanted to belong to something so badly. Coach Kirsch was tough, but he knew when someone really needed a lifeline, so he let me ride the bench, even though I often couldn't even finish practices because of the pain.

Despite all this, one refuge I did not seek was alcohol or drugs. My dad drank, and I was so determined to be nothing like him, I swore off alcohol completely. Avoiding drugs was a no brainer, as I felt steering clear of them might give me a competitive edge on the basketball court.

In my final year of high school, I had an experience whose significance wasn't clear at the time. It all started with my being an insufferable smart-ass in Joan Kane's Spanish class.

Ms. Kane—the third teacher who greatly influenced me—was very pretty and very unwilling to put up with my shenanigans. I was a discipline problem for her, just to get her attention. Poor Ms. Kane, though, had no other tools at her disposal but to give me one after-school detention slip after another, which was of course exactly what I wanted; it prolonged my time with her because detention, fortuitously, was held in her classroom. Though I cringe to remember it, I was so far gone that I'd write her platonic Shakespearean love notes suggesting that someday, when I was older, maybe she could see me differently . . .

One day during detention Ms. Kane stationed me at a desk as far from her as possible and handed me a pile of pamphlets. She was involved in some charity, apparently, and she wanted me to see what it was about. That would be my punishment, to read the pamphlets. I shuffled through them. They'd been issued by an organization called Amnesty International and another called Bread for the World. I'd never heard of either one.

For the next hour I looked at pictures and read stories of people who were starving, who had been tortured, who were child soldiers, who were refugees, and who had experienced other atrocities that hit me right in the stomach. The misery I'd seen at the shelter in Philly or Times Square was nothing compared to what was going on in Africa. *This* was injustice on an operatic scale. *This* was unfairness.

It wasn't an immediate change-your-life moment. I was too self-absorbed for that. But those images got squirreled away somewhere deep inside my adolescent brain and would, a few years later, end up changing my life.

All of these experiences led me to a very nocturnal, insomnia-fueled, internally focused productivity, evidenced by a growing collection of marble notebooks, dozens of them, angst-filled reflections overflowing every page of every book. These were my journals chronicling my high school tribulations. The amazing thing is that an entry would be dated July 15, 1980, 8 P.M., and there would be a few pages of writing. Then July 15, midnight, and there'd be a couple more. Then July 16, 1980, 2 A.M., and there would be three more. I was utterly consumed. And I barely made it out of high school; my grades—due to neglect and disinterest—descended in a free fall, and my behavior, attitude, and emotional state were not far behind. But make it out

I did, and finally I went off to college in Washington, D.C., at Georgetown University. Free of my father, at last.

In my obsessive, guilt-ridden way, I became a total grind during my debt-filled freshman year at Georgetown University. While everybody else in the dorm was out drinking and partying, I'd be on the third floor of the library, consuming book after book unrelated to my course work with a voraciousness that, in retrospect, seems fairly desperate. There was too much injustice in the world for a guilty Catholic sinner like me to take a minute off. In my lonely, bruised state, I really believed it was partly up to me to rid the world of injustice. In order to get that done, I was going to have to learn all I could about how the world works.

I had a roommate in the dorm, a smart and charismatic guy named Geoff Mills, and I never let the poor fella sleep. Either I was clacking away on my little portable typewriter writing long-winded papers at the last minute, or I was keeping him up with arguments about Kerouac's *On the Road,* or Tolstoy's *War and Peace,* to a sound track of Bob Dylan songs. I slept only a few hours a night; I had an alarm clock on which I wrote "Wake Up You Hopeless Wretch" and left it deliberately on an overturned steel garbage can across the room so that the can would amplify the alarm and I'd have to get out of bed to shut it off and get back to my reading.

Urban poverty was still my obsession, so I signed on with a Georgetown program run by my buddy Dan Porterfield that sent volunteers to teach reading to kids in the projects in one of the low-income African-American neighborhoods in D.C., the section of the city you don't see in the tourist promotional materials and the monuments. I roped my roommate Geoff into some of those expeditions; we'd have to wear these bright orange vests, and we would be let off at night outside these ominous high-rise towers, abominations of some social engineering experiment of decades gone by. Walking down the dark corridors and venturing into those airless, dilapidated apartments was, for me, a passageway to finding my purpose; I felt I was approaching ground zero of America's need.

Another important friend during freshman year was the guy who ultimately led me directly to Michael: John Kaiser. John was British, with a fair complexion and pink cheeks, and he slept in his sleeping bag the entire year, ready to leave Georgetown at a moment's notice; we called him "the dawg." John and I fancied ourselves the social conscience of the dorm. Everybody else was going to use their Georgetown degrees to become investment bankers, we believed, but he and I were going to help save the world.

One perversely positive thing happened during freshman year. I discovered the miracle cure for acne: Accutane. I took them as religiously as if they were birth control pills. They dried my skin so completely that it created incredible flaking, but at least it eliminated the cysts that had been my mask since the onset of the hurricane otherwise known as puberty. I have a vague memory of beginning my transformation from the ugly duckling I thought I was destined to be, but I studiously paid no attention at all, as absorbed as I was in my learning.

I did, however, take a small emotional chance on a young lady who I had become close with during my senior year in high school, an equally socially awkward student-athlete with whom I used to take all-night walks in our Pennsylvania neighborhood the summer before Georgetown, tentatively sharing our pain and our dreams. We began some form of long-distance full-fledged dating in the fall semester. During Christmas break, I was driving around with some of my old basketball team, and one of the guys told me that he had seen my girlfriend holding hands with another guy. A little research unearthed that she had been seeing him the entire time I thought we were together. What shred of self-esteem I had begun to build in the early stages of life without acne was smashed on the rocks. I went back into my cave and didn't come back out for a long, long time. I emerged, strangely, as a guy who was almost bizarrely confident, but only in superficial encounters with women, devoid of intimacy and as self-protective as a porcupine, so certain of my inability to be loved for who I was.

I was too restless to stay at Georgetown, and I wanted desperately to discover my country for myself. So I dropped out after that first year and went off on a kind of hitchhiking expedition trying to absorb as much real world knowledge and experience as I could. I remained an enigma to my parents, who genuinely worried that I was drifting dangerously toward some kind of bad outcome that they couldn't imagine but could fear.

For part of the time, I hitchhiked around working on various political campaigns in Los Angeles, Phoenix, Albuquerque, and finally Chicago (where Harold Washington was seeking to become that city's first African-American mayor), trying to better understand how our political system works. In between campaigns, I was on the road with my thumb out, going from place to place, talking with everyone, and living out of a tent and a backpack. I also went to Texas and cut across the border to Mexico to learn about labor issues from a tough old union organizer and Latino advocate named Jack Ortega, alternatively nicknamed "El Tigre" and the "con man for the people."

But the stretch in San Francisco in the fall of 1982 was particularly meaningful because of three role models who laid the foundation for the monumental life choices I was to make a year later. Patrick Goggins, Paul Comiskey, and Johnny Maher. Three Irish guys, all blazing a trail so bright for social justice that they eliminated any doubts I might have had about whether one person can make a difference.

Mr. Goggins was my Georgetown dorm-mate Billy's dad. When I showed up at his doorstep in the late summer of 1982, Pat Goggins and his wife Ute welcomed me with open arms. He told me that first week that I had wild eyes and I talked so Philly-tough that he thought I had some broken cartilage in my tongue. Mr. Goggins had worked on civil rights issues in the sixties and Native American causes in the seventies, but he had now focused on what he could do to contribute to solutions in the place of his heritage, Northern Ireland. A law encyclopedia salesman, he set up an organization, the Irish Forum, which aimed to get beyond the polarization between the Catholics and the Protestants there and discuss solutions to the challenges Northern Ireland faced. His work emboldened those back in Belfast who were courageous enough to chart a course toward peaceful coexistence, and it helped neutralize some of the hard-core sentiments back in the United States for one side or the other. An encyclopedia salesman in California contributing to peace in Northern Ireland!

Mr. Goggins introduced me to Father Paul Comiskey, a Jesuit priest and lawyer who wore all black and cowboy boots as if he were Johnny Cash or something. Father Paul took on as his ministry the battle against the death penalty and a campaign to improve the shockingly bad conditions of the residents of California's penal institutions. He helped form the Prisoners' Union, and he would visit people in prison, advocate for their rights and for smarter policies (serving bad food and having poor prison health care ends up INCREASING costs to the state, not decreasing them), and help with their cases. (The quality of public defense is shockingly bad or even nonexistent in many cases, leading to a situation in which the accused are effectively deprived of counsel, even though the right to defense counsel is a basic hallmark of our justice system.) Father Paul focused on the individual, the person, the human being who—yes—had been accused or convicted of a crime but still deserved to be treated with dignity and fairness, and who was more than the worst thing he or she had ever done.

If Mr. Goggins and Father Paul weren't enough to inspire me, I had been reading a book about a guy called John Maher, the co-founder of the Delancey Street Foundation, a cutting-edge rehabilitation program for people fighting addictions, overcoming homelessness, or reentering society after incarceration. John Maher was also the subject of a *60 Minutes* episode that so enthralled me that I went to his office one morning wearing the Irish scally cap that was my trademark that whole year, and sat in the lobby all day hoping for a chance to meet him. Eight hours passed, and they told me I had to leave because they were closing up, so I came back the next morning and waited again.

Finally, that afternoon the doors burst open and there he was, Johnny Maher, arm in arm with Cesar Chavez, the legendary farmworker activist. He looked at me and said, "So you're the kid who won't leave, huh?" And with that he signaled me to follow him, and for two weeks he let me shadow him around San Francisco, attending labor meetings with Chavez, political rallies, clandestine fundraising events for Northern Ireland's independence, and inspirational speeches he would make to the residents at Delancey Street. Johnny, as people called him, never asked me a question, including my name, but he never stopped talking to me either. He dispensed some of the most motivating advice and stories I have ever heard or read, infiltrating my head and heart with the simple idea that no injustice should be allowed to stand, and that if it wasn't for us to confront it, then who?

Meeting these huge personalities, these social reformers who saw injustice in the world and had the moxy to think they themselves could change it, taught me to be undeterred by tough odds, and it taught me that an individual can make a difference and that we should see the world as we want it to be and work like hell to make it come true. I even began writing a column entitled *The Way We Will* for the University of San Francisco paper.

I was drinking from the fire hose of life, but all in a hit-and-run manner. This applied to my education, volunteer work, jobs, and relationships. I'd work a little bit at some internship or soup kitchen and then move on. I'd take classes at one college and then move on to another, working in odd jobs to make enough money to survive, with an occasional "loan" from my baffled parents. I was a grazer, a nomad, constantly moving on to the next thing to learn a little more, but never making any kind of emotional attachment to anything. My instinctive impulse, as always, continued to be well-guarded withdrawal.

I still felt deeply misunderstood, so not only did I bounce from project to project and school to school in a rapacious ramble to learn and move on but I also veered away from the precipice of intimacy. I went through a lot of short-term girlfriends in those days, and I remember now with sadness that I wasn't sufficiently concerned with other people's feelings. I was angry, hurt, and much too self-absorbed.

The universe, though, abhors imbalance, and it has a way of sending us exactly what we need, even if it isn't what we want. As the summer of 1983 began, I unexpectedly heard from my old Georgetown buddy John Kaiser, the dawg himself, who said he was overseeing a homeless shelter on Fourteenth Street in D.C., near a corner marked by prostitution, drug dealing, and public drunkenness. I went up there one day to visit him, and nothing's been the same since.

It is life's most random moments—its chance meetings—that can be the most profound ones.

MICHAEL MATTOCKS

Those Hefty bags, man, I'll never forget that. We must have stayed in every shelter in the District of Columbia twice over.

There was one shelter at Fourteenth and N, right across the street from a big-ass church. It was a townhouse, red brick, and there was a big room on the top floor with lots of cots in it. This white dude named John Kaiser kind of ran the place. He wore shorts and flip-flops and had a room off to the side that wasn't much better than ours. He slept in a sleeping bag on a ratty old couch with his cool Russian girlfriend named Kashi. I remember he used to let me and James look for coins in the sofa cushions.

One day me and James go tearing in there—I was about

seven, James six—and there's this other white dude in there. He was tall and wiry, with kind of rough skin on his face and a short beard that ran around the bottom of his chin. Right away I could tell this white man was different. I was used to grownups towering over me and kind of talking down at me, but this guy got down on the floor by me and James so his eyes were at our own level. And he used a different voice than other grownups used, not like he was telling us to do something—or stop doing something—but like he was interested in what we had to say. Man, he was full of questions! "What's your name?" "How many brothers and sisters you got?" "Where do you go to school?" "What's your favorite subject?" "You like basketball?" I'd answer one, and he'd be off to the next. I'd never had a grownup so interested in me before; it was kind of funny. Then I remember he asked me a really weird question. He said, "Do you know how to read?"

Read? I was only seven years old! So this white dude, a guy I never saw before, asks if me and James want to go to the library, that minute, and learn how to read.

That was how I met J.P. I guess he asked my mom if he could take us out, and when I think about it, it's strange she said yes. I mean, she didn't know this white dude either. He was just some stranger, and he could have taken us anywhere. She liked John Kaiser, though, and trusted him. If this white dude was a friend of his, then he must be okay. Next thing I knew, him and me and James were out there onto Fourteenth Street together.

It was all whores up there back then, and man, some of them were fine! Little as I was, I used to love sitting out there on the stoop and watching them. J.P. asked us if we'd eaten that day, and I'm sure we probably had, but it probably hadn't been anything but cereal, or peanut butter on bread, or some chips. We was always ready to eat, and J.P. took and got us a McDonald's. Then we walked up to this little library they had up there. Not the big Martin Luther King library; I guess it was a branch. In a townhouse. Beautiful inside there, and quiet in a way I wasn't used to. Like, *thick* quiet. J.P. sat there with us going through books, trying to teach us how to read. We hunched over the books, J.P.'s finger sliding along under the words, and I'd steal little glances sideways. His face was down close to mine, with that rough skin all over it. He'd be all focused on the book, and on me, like nothing else existed in the world. I remember thinking: Who is this white dude? Why is he doing this? Why does he care?

Left to right: Sabrina, Elsie, Denise, André, Michael, and David

JOHN PRENDERGAST

John's shelter was a tall townhouse. The street outside was raucous. Back then on Fourteenth Street, right there on the corner of that homeless shelter, the prostitutes openly paraded their wares while other people offered all kinds of illicit paraphernalia for sale. The top floor was almost entirely one big room full of beds; John had a small room of his own in the corner. He and his Russian girlfriend, Kashi, shared that same ratty sleeping bag from his days at Georgetown on a couch that was covered with cat hair and cigarette burns; he hadn't changed a bit. It was great seeing him still involved in the struggle, trying to bring some peace and dignity to people who were temporarily without a home. The Reagan Revolution was in full budget-cutting flower at this point, and John and I immediately launched into an intense discussion about the infuriating indignities we felt it was inflicting on poorer households—both the withdrawal of funding for services and also the chronic demonization of poor people as lazy and immoral. We were thick into our discussion when suddenly two tiny boys came tearing into John's room like a pair of little tornadoes. The older one was seven; he had a big round caramel-colored face and the brightest and widest eyes I'd ever seen. The younger one, six, was skinny and darker, and he didn't move more than three inches from the side of his big brother. My friend John made them slow down a second and introduce themselves. "Michael," the big one said, pointing to his own chest with a pudgy finger. "This is James, my brother."

He ain't heavy, father.

They asked John if they could look through his sofa cushions for dropped change, to which he said yes, and they went at it like a couple of gold miners.

I'd been around a lot of kids by then. I'd met children from all sorts of backgrounds at the shelters in Philadelphia and New York, in the projects during my freshman year at Georgetown, and coaching youth basketball teams. Up until then, the kids were never fully three-dimensional individuals to me, but instead they were symbols of something bigger—of poverty, of the inadequate way city governments delivered services, of rotten school systems, of absent fathers. This day, though, I found myself staring at these two little boys as though encountering something entirely new. A light came off them—particularly off the older one, Michael—that just about blinded me. He seemed to glow with a cheerfulness and optimism that was totally counterintuitive given his circumstances. I mean, these boys had *nothing* and yet radiated with life and sunshine.

As they rooted around in the couch, John took me out into the main room to meet their mother, Denise. She was pretty, and she had a certain dignified air about her, but she also seemed as overwhelmed and exhausted as anyone I had ever met. Their things were strewn around their cots, spilling out of big black Hefty bags that they'd obviously been living out of and lugging through the streets.

By the time we got back to John's room, the boys had started shooting hoops with balls of paper into the trash can, interspersed with vigorous wrestling. It was like watching a couple of lion cubs rolling around on each other. Here I'd been studying the effects of poverty on children and these two seemed utterly unaffected by it. The word that comes to mind is *undefeated*; they were completely joyful in the moment. I sat down on the floor to bring my face down to their level, and when Michael turned that big moon face of his at me, it was like a burst of unexpected sunshine.

I began doing the thing my dad used to do—firing questions. "Do you go to school? What do you like about it? What don't you like about it? What's your favorite food? What's your favorite TV show? What's your favorite basketball team? What's your favorite football team? What's your favorite baseball team? Why? Why do you like them? Who's your favorite player?" Questions, questions, questions—it didn't even matter what they were, just a constant stream of stimuli in the hopes of getting something back. Michael, the older one, was very sparkly and eager to please. It was clear he loved having all this adult attention turned on him. He was a little bewildered, but he did his best to keep up. James, on the other hand, hung back. He was more wary, and a little sneakier too. He tried to get his little hand into my pocket. Then he took a pair of scissors from John's desk. Not bad things, really. Just sneaky.

"Hey," I heard myself say. "You guys know how to read?"

They lit up and laughed as though I was Bill Cosby, their faces a riot of pink tongues and white teeth. I may as well have asked them if they could fly. "I'm serious," I said. "If you want, I'll take you to the library and teach you to read."

"Right now?" Michael piped, his eyes wide, and I thought, well, sure. Why not? Why not right now? I walked out into the main room and found Denise.

"Is it okay with you if I take the boys out for a little while?" I asked. "I thought I'd take them over to the library and teach them a little bit about reading."

She looked up at me with eyes so exhausted they seemed varnished, and I could see her making all the calculations: Who is this white man? What's he want with my boys? She'd have seen a wiry guy with a rough, pock-marked face hidden by a sharply trimmed dark beard. She also, apparently, saw something she trusted.

She knew my buddy John; he'd been kind to her. And maybe my suggestion that I, a perfect stranger, immediately take her kids to read at the library was so strange that no self-respecting kidnapper or child molester would think of such a thing. She agreed to let me take the boys for a few hours. Michael and James scampered down the stairs two at a time. Something different! Something new! We didn't so much walk to the library as play our way there. Who can jump up and touch that sign? Who can leap frog over the fire hydrant? Who can find a leaf with the most red in it? Who can walk backward the farthest without falling down? I was being my dad—every kid's clown. They were so hungry for play that we'd finish up one little game and they'd be, "What's next? What's next?"

The nearest library was a pretty little branch office in a brownstone, and I got down on one knee to explain that we couldn't play in there, that it's a library where people go to read quietly. I was a little nervous taking them in there; they were so busy and noisy and full of energy. I figured it would take about two minutes for us to get thrown out. But the two of them—tiny little guys, holding hands—walked in there like explorers happening on some elaborate underground golden temple. Their eyes rolled around as we tip-toed through, utterly rapt at all the books, the shiny polished wood, the immaculate, learned silence that enveloped the room. I sat them at a table and retrieved a picture book, and they fixated on it as though it was a magical artifact from another dimension. The boys had to have seen books in school, but I got the impression that nobody had ever sat with them and thoroughly directed their attention into one. They turned the pages with their mouths hanging open, visibly dumbstruck by some of the stories I was reading them.

I started teaching them how to sound out the letters, and it was a whole new game for them. If I expected them to resist, I couldn't have been more wrong, because making sounds out of the squiggles on the page was as fresh and fun as crab walking on the grass or playing "I Spy." Watching them puzzling over how a *t* and an *h* together make that hissing sound, or the way one makes an *o* with one's lips when making the sound of the letter, I felt as though I was watching a fast-motion film of seeds landing on fertile earth, germinating and sprouting into green shoots. Michael and James had such fresh, ready, unspoiled minds—despite what must have been such a disorienting and sometimes harrowing experience as living from shelter to shelter—that my heart began banging around inside my chest. Until this moment, I'd been focused on the problems of poverty, and I hadn't allowed myself to think about actual solutions for real people. But watching Michael and James, I found myself thinking: Anything is possible.

I was taking them page by page through a children's book. I felt lucky that I could introduce them to a world of pictures and words that had fired my imagination when I was their age. On one page was a picture of a family standing outside their house, and before I could turn to the next, Michael slapped his plump little hand down on it. "I'm going to get my mom a house," he said in a low tone I hadn't heard before. I look over at him, and his face had utterly changed. His eyebrows, which had ridden excitedly around his hairline all day, were scrunched down around his nose. He looked, suddenly, like a tiny grownup. "Someday *soon*, I'm going to buy my mom a house and take care of our family."

"Michael," I said. "You're just a kid."

Michael (left) and James

"That don't matter," he said. He looked at the picture a long time, and then slowly turned the page. His face relaxed, the eyebrows floated up. After another couple of pages, he was back to his smiley self, and that dark little interlude might never have happened.

From there I took them to McDonald's to fill up their bellies for a couple bucks, which is probably all I had in my pocket at the time, and then back to the shelter. They thundered up the stairs yelling to their mother about all the things they'd done, and I went in to John's room to say goodbye. Before I could leave, Michael came bouncing over and grabbed my hand. "When you coming back?" he asked, his shiny face tilted up toward mine. "When we doing this again?"

2. "Come to Save the Day"

MICHAEL MATTOCKS

Every time we moved from one shelter to another that summer, I'd worry that J.P. wouldn't be able to find us. But then one day, there he'd be. I don't know how he found us every time; he'd just show up, and off we'd go. It was like being with a big kid; he'd make up little games as we walked along, duck-walking and one-foot hopping. For the longest time he had this ugly station wagon, kind of a tan color, and he'd put me and James in the back and drive us around. We'd usually go get a McDonald's or a Roy Rogers or a Pizza Hut, because we were always hungry, and then to the library. It was funny; I couldn't have cared less about learning to read in school, but with J.P. it was fun. We'd sit up at one of those long tables, the three of us, and go through book after book.

The best thing we did, though, was fishing. We'd go down to the Potomac, back behind the Watergate Hotel. J.P. always had these busted-up rods. There was a little business back there, Thompson Boats, that had a vending machine where you'd put in quarters and out would come little cups of dirt with worms in them, for bait. J.P., James, and I would stand on the docks catching catfish, rockfish, even striped bass. We wouldn't keep them, though—you didn't want to eat fish out of that nasty-ass river. We'd throw them back.

Right across from Thompson Boats was an island, maybe half a mile long, with no houses or roads on it or nothing. Just woods. Sometimes when J.P. had a little money, he'd rent a canoe or a rowboat, and we'd go over there—we had to row like a motherfucker to keep from getting carried off by the current—and we'd play explorers or Indians or something out there all damn day. J.P. got totally into playing like a kid. Not like some adults who just go along with it and get tired right quick. J.P. got *into* it. He became a kid when he was with us.

At the same time, though, J.P. always had books with him, always had big stacks of papers and files. He'd fish a while with me and James, or play, and then I'd look over and he'd be sitting on a rock with a book open. Sometimes he'd take us back to his apartment, which wasn't any nicer than the shelter, really, and we'd eat Honey Combs and play around, and J.P. would be in on his little typewriter with all these books open all around him. Man, he'd be going at it. He'd be working those books and that typewriter as hard as he played with us. We'd let him at it a while, and then we'd say, "Hey, J.P., take a break." He'd jump up and come play with us for an hour—roll around on the floor wrestling, or playing hide-and-seek out in the streets. Then I'd look up and J.P. would have his nose back in those books, or he'd be banging at his typewriter.

Sooner or later he'd take us home, and the day would be over. J.P. would drive off, and we wouldn't know if we'd ever see him again. Sometimes it felt like our times with J.P. was a dream, like they weren't real.

We had relatives in Southeast D.C., and we'd go out there

sometimes when we were homeless. When I was about eight or nine, my mom found us a place to live on Savannah Terrace in Southeast. I don't really know how she did it, but it was nice down there, even though we were ten people living in a two-room apartment: Mom, me, and my brothers and sisters Sabrina, James, David, Elsie, André (who was born in the shelter), two of Aunt Evelyn's kids, and Uncle Artie. Sabrina, James, and I could ride our bikes down to the river, and throw rocks, catch tadpoles—and crayfish the size of lobsters! There were backyards, and parks, where we'd play football. I taught James how to catch big-ass bees off them flowering bushes; we'd trap them in bottles. There were plum trees we'd climb to get plums, and apple trees we'd pick apples from.

James and I were always together. I could beat him up because I was bigger, but he'd always get me back; I could count on that. Like I said before, James had a temper on him, even when he was a little kid. Take something off him, pick him last for a team, even look at him the wrong way, and he'd go off. It didn't bother me when we were little; that's just how James was. Later on, I made use of that side of James; I'll admit that. Now I just wish I'd been able to turn that side of him off.

Sabrina was still no joke either. There was this boy named Quinton one day that was bullying me and James in a way Sabrina didn't like. He had this slingshot hanging around his neck, and Sabrina grabbed it, pulled it way back, and let it go. Then for good measure, while old Quinton was gasping and choking, Sabrina ran inside and got a big-ass butcher knife. She probably would have stuck it in him if we hadn't pulled her off. Sabrina wasn't but about ten years old at the time.

It's good James and Sabrina were tough that way, because while we were living down there, the Jamaicans starting moving in, and they were bad motherfuckers. It was like they all arrived at once; suddenly the streets were full of them. They were trying to take over, and them niggers down in Southeast weren't having any of it. There was a lot of killing around then. One summer day Sabrina, James, and I were walking down a side street near our apartment and smelled something nasty. We look up, and there's a dead body sitting in a parked car right there. Hot as a motherfucker and this guy's all swole up behind the wheel.

I used to have dreams about that. I'd see that swollen up man, and then he'd turn his head and look at me. At night, that shit would snap me right out of bed.

Our uncle Artie came to live with us down in Southeast; his wife had died of cancer up in New Jersey, and he was all by himself. He was scary and funny at the same time. He drank pretty much all day, but that was normal for people in my family. We were never afraid of him because we knew he was harmless. He always had pockets full of snacks, and he'd play games with us, reaching out for our faces and saying, "Gimme that eeeeeeye," and "Gimme that noooooooose." Bony, skinny motherfucker was Artie; a good dude. You could sit in a room and talk to him and he'd listen, even if he didn't know what it was you were talking about. I used to watch him give himself insulin shots.

Uncle Artie didn't work, but nobody we knew worked. My mom wasn't working at all then. She wasn't into the drugs, and I'm not sure she was even drinking then; that came later. But it's not like anybody was looking after us kids; we'd make ourselves a sandwich for dinner. I don't think one person in our whole family had a decent job. Everybody was always freeloading off of somebody else, conning a little money off them, nobody pulling their own weight. Looking back on it now, it was fucked up. We kids didn't have one grownup in the entire family we could look up to and see how to live right. And I wasn't but about eight, nine years old then.

People in Southeast would come up to me and say, "Tell your father 'hi.' I grew up with him." At first, I thought they were talking about Willie, but after a while I started piecing it together that they were talking about somebody else. The somebody else they were talking about had been a prizefighter. People would say to me, "Your dad knocked me out; holler at him for me." I figured out too that he was a gambler, a stone gangster. I even had a guy come up and say, "Your dad, he shot me one time; you tell him 'hi' for me." That shit confused me.

One day there were people over at the house for some kind of party. The door opened and I looked over. A man I'd never seen stood there. He was dressed snappy—slacks and a white shirt, with a tan leather jacket and a fedora hat. I heard my aunt whisper to someone, "That's their dad," but I knew it already, the second I saw him. When I seen him, I seen me. Except for recently, my whole life I'd thought Willie was my dad, and this stranger walks in and I know right away that he's my real father. I don't know why he showed up right then; I guess he was waiting until we had a place he could stay. He had that I-don't-give-a-fuck attitude. He stayed that day and lived with us for about a minute—just long enough to get my mother pregnant with Tyrell. Me and Sabrina, at the start of the lineup, and Tyrell, at the tail end, we all had the same father. James, David, and Elsie were Willie's children. André was born in 1984 while we were in the shelter; I don't know who the hell his father is. It's not like any of these dudes was around. My dad was gone again as slick and easy as he'd come.

I was hurt, I really was. It was so good having my dad around. He bought us beds and a kitchen table. He was tough too. I really looked up to him. One day my mom and him got in a really big argument, and he left right then. I felt like a big part of us just left.

And suddenly out of nowhere, J.P. would appear there on Savannah Terrace. Even though my dad left, we had J.P. We was so happy when he would come. That big ugly car of his would roll up, and we'd be off on another one of our adventures. Busting out of that house with J.P. was like getting air into our lungs. It wasn't just fun. It was good for us. J.P. did shit with his life, you hear what I'm saying? He had things going on—jobs, and school. And he cared about us in a way even my mom and my aunts didn't know how to. He'd ask us about our lives, and talk to us about things like being responsible, and working hard, and setting our sights on dreams and shit like that. Nobody in our world talked to us about that. And here's the thing: J.P. didn't judge us. He didn't judge my mom or Uncle Artie. They was what they was, and J.P. accepted that.

My aunts would say to my mom, "Why you letting that white man go with your kids?" and my mom would say, "He

Left to right: James, David, Michael, Tyrell, Denise, and Elsie

ain't doing nothing to them kids." My mom loved us, and she knew what was best even if she couldn't always do what was best. She never said we couldn't go with J.P. There was something about J.P. she trusted. And I think my aunts were jealous, and maybe Mom liked that a little bit. James and me, we'd come back saying, "We did this! We did that." Had our bellies all full; sometimes we even had on new shoes.

There were times back then that I didn't want to be around where I was at all. What I really wanted was to be living with J.P.

JOHN PRENDERGAST

My peculiar upbringing had both set me up for this relationship with Michael and James and also left me completely unprepared for it. I was a white, middle-class American. My nuclear family hadn't split up. I had a supportive extended family. I was blessed with the ability to attend the country's best universities. To bend all that advantage toward promoting myself—to get rich for its own sake—was unthinkable. I walked around as my skull rang, twenty-four hours a day, with a humanistic and theological compulsion to add value to the world. I was finally the big boy in the Boys' Town tableau, ready to carry the little one uncomplainingly on my back. In my head, I was the comic book-turned-real-life superhero, come to help save the day.

But notice: I was really all about me—how *I* was going to learn about the poor, how *I* was going to redeem myself through service, how *I* was going to be the superhero. Often the people who needed help were more like props in my play.

I was spreading myself incredibly thin that summer of 1983—taking courses at George Washington University, working at the Robert Kennedy Memorial Youth Policy Institute, volunteering as a kids' basketball coach. It was as though I couldn't do enough to fight unfairness, or stuff my head fast enough with information and experience about urban poverty and its causes. Was I doing any good? Maybe not; I didn't stay with anything long enough. And was I learning? Perhaps in some superficial way. But I'd driven myself into such a frenzy of activity that it was almost as though the point wasn't to do good or learn; the point was to check off boxes. Did this, did this, did this, did this . . .

And maybe also to feed this growing addiction to achievement, as well as the increasing tendency to fill the hole in my heart with spiraling amounts of frenetic activity, never stopping long enough to let the demons of loneliness and lack of self-worth catch up to me.

In a way, it was a terrible burden. Work had become a compulsion I couldn't control, and it was driving me to do things I really didn't feel like doing. I was twenty years old; I wanted to play basketball all day. I wanted to sit on the couch and watch sports. I wanted to be a sportswriter, not a saint. And the more I felt myself yearning to relax, have fun, enjoy my own life, the more I felt compelled to add one more task of service to my already overloaded dance card. And even that served my overheated and guilt-ridden sense of self: The more I denied myself, the more I jammed in another book, another course, another little piece of service work, the more self-righteous I felt.

At first, I simply folded my relationship with Michael and James into this spin cycle of feverish service. It was the injustice of their circumstances that drew me in—how they could never seem to get out of the shelters. The issues were legion: unmet criteria; late buses; unsympathetic program officers. The list went on and on. The thing the family probably needed most from me I had none of: money.

Denise was full of contrasts, and no stereotype would ever capture her completely. She was the ultimate mother hen, taking in children from her extended family even when she was living in a homeless shelter. But she was also overwhelmed by the responsibility of caring for all these little kids on her own. So at times my guess is she retreated into heavy drinking to cope. But she never let go of her kids' hands. She was fantastically devoted to them.

Getting to know Michael and James made me want to learn more about homelessness in general. It turns out that most people that go to shelters aren't the folks with mental illnesses that we usually see in the streets. That's a very small percentage. Most are families or individuals who have lost jobs, are battling drug or alcohol addictions, or have come out of prison with no support structures. Nearly half of the people who spend time at shelters have worked in the past thirty days. That has always blown me away. Shelters are definitely the last safety net, but the system is full of gaping holes and crushing indignities for the people in them, and not enough has been done over the years to address the root causes in terms of developing treatment programs, employment opportunities, and subsidized permanent housing. If, as they say, a society should be judged for the quality of mercy for its least fortunate, America has a long way to go.

When they finally did get an apartment, down in Southeast D.C., their old Uncle Artie came to live off of them. He was about the skinniest man I've ever seen, and completely spaced out all the time. Near as I could tell, he didn't do anything but sit in the house and drink all day. He was the friendliest parasitic fella I'd ever met; if the boys had fifteen cents in their pockets, he'd figure a way to get it off them so he could get something to drink, and do it all with a smile. Michael and James were probably eating every day, but it's not like it was always at the same time and with the same people, and most of the time it was probably cereal, chips, or white bread out of the package with a little peanut butter.

The boys didn't have one single positive role model in their entire life. I had this idea that having gotten to them early enough, I could show them a positive way to be a man. And that I could do it in a way that wouldn't cost me anything. I thought I could swoop in, make a splash, do something of lasting value, and get out without much personal responsibility on my part—sort of a rent-a-dad.

A part of me thought that I could use Michael and James to correct my father's mistakes. I told myself that unlike my dad, I would appreciate the boys for who they were instead of creating some impossible ideal in my mind that would constantly be disabused by reality. And I would stick by them no matter what they did or what they became, I thought. My father may not have been able to deal with it when I became a teenager, as so many parents can't, but I'd be bigger than that. I'd be smarter. I'd be more compassionate.

In retrospect, it seems that yet another way I was using my relationship with Michael and James for my own gratification was that for the first time in my life, I wanted to be *seen*. I'd spent so many years hiding—in the bushes, in the neighbor's garage, in the basement, behind towels—that I'd forgotten how good it could feel to be visible. When Michael, James, and I were out on the street, you couldn't *not* look at us; we were like a circus barreling along—running, jumping, shouting, throwing balls in the air. And I was loving it. I felt needed by the boys, and for the first time I really wanted to be visible.

So there I was, checking off boxes, earnestly rubbing my guilt-inflamed Catholic martyr's ego up against the problems of the world, externalizing and intellectualizing everything, and Michael and James did an end run around all that and completely unmanned me. I'd go to pick them up, they'd gaze up at me with those eager faces of theirs, and something inside my chest would simply dissolve. They were the first people I'd encountered who were thoroughly nonjudgmental; they didn't see acne scars or any of my other flaws, and they didn't measure my performance. They were just kids, wanting to go out and play. And unlike everybody else I encountered, Michael and James were completely available to be nurtured. Against my will I was finding that they were stirring up a part of me that I'd let atrophy all those dark years. I'd grown a thick skin against everything, it turned out, but unconditional love. They directed a big fat beam of it at me and knocked me right over.

I found myself, for the first time, not skipping off to the next thing. I found myself looking forward to seeing them, to heading down to Southeast D.C. not to punch my ticket, and not out of any kind of save-the-world altruism, but because I couldn't wait to have fun with those little guys again. Some of the neighbors down in Southeast told me they thought I was a cop. What other white guy would come down there? I was driving the ugliest car ever built—a big beige station wagon my buddies called "the fleshmobile." I'd load the boys into that, drive over to our favorite getaway, and we'd get out there on the

Potomac River with our fishing rods, or go ramming around in the woods on the island. After all the hard work I was doing, being with the boys I'd completely lose myself in being a kid. With nobody judging me. Nobody expressing disappointment in me. With Michael and James I could enjoy brother-play in a way I'd never done with Luke. I felt like a fist unclenching for the first time.

One thing I learned early on was that even though they had let him down in every way you can think of, Michael was, naturally, absolutely committed to his family. If I asked something like, "Did anybody feed you today?" Michael would peel back his little shoulders, looking like he was ready to throw down. "My mom's got it hard," he'd say. "She's doing the best she can." He never blamed her, never held anything against her. He even defended Uncle Artie to me; said he was a good listener. Artie!

Michael would bring it up again and again. We'd be fishing, or lying on our backs in the park looking at clouds, and he'd suddenly say, "I'm going to get my family settled someplace. I'm going to get them a house, someplace they'll be safe." Eight years old! I guess being the oldest son in a family like that, he could have gone one of two ways. He could easily have said, Screw it, I'm going to do like what I see around me and just get mine. Instead, though, he drew the opposite lesson, that he was going to do well and support his family when he got the chance. How he planned to learn a better way was a mystery to me. He had nobody to look up to around him. I mean, I held jobs and all, but I was not the greatest child-rearing role model.

James was more of a puzzle than Michael. Michael was sweet all the time—open and trusting. James, though, . . . James kept a part of himself guarded. We'd have fun together, and James would play and be as giggly and rambunctious as any kid. But

part of him would hang back; he wouldn't engage with me as deeply and as willingly as Michael did.

And then there was his temper, which was genuinely scary. James would be smiling and joking one moment, and the next he'd be a damned dervish, swinging his fists with reckless abandon. Often I wouldn't even know what set it off. We'd be fishing, or throwing a football around in a park, or climbing on a jungle-gym somewhere, having a great time, and suddenly James would be whaling the stuffings out of some poor kid on the playground. I'd have to pull him off. Later, I'd try to deconstruct what had happened, and it was always something tiny. A kid fouled him playing basketball. Another kid taunted him from the top of the jungle-gym. Somebody grabbed a bite of his popsicle without asking. Each time, it seemed, the thing that set James off was some slight, some tiny gesture of disrespect—something that any other kid, like Michael, would probably let go. James couldn't let anything go.

James had a real feeling of aggrievedness in him—a deep, tortured sense of having been wronged. Somebody in the family told me that James had been abused when he was really young, but I didn't know any details, and I never confirmed the story. Kids who act out in this way often have suffered trauma and abuse. I'd try to ask Michael and Denise about it, but they'd evade the questions. All I ever heard was what a good man James' father Willie had been before he got sick and wandered off. Still, I couldn't help wondering. The wounds in James were so fresh, so painful, and so close to the surface.

That summer of 1983, I was supporting myself by working weekends with a family of Russian-American landscapers in Philadelphia, related to my buddy Nick, one of my old high

school basketball teammates. I'd race up I-95 on Friday from D.C. and bust sod in the hot sun all weekend. The work was hard, but it was cold cash, and two days of it would support a week of living like a monk in D.C. I'd stay with my parents while in Philly, despite the fact that I was still not on speaking terms with my dad. The yelling had lessened, but the volcano was smoldering; I simply refused to acknowledge he existed.

One weekend I asked Denise if the boys could come with me. For some reason James couldn't go, but Michael was available and he was eager for anything. Denise said sure. I'm sure she was glad to have at least one of them out from underfoot for a couple of days. By that time, she also had Elsie, who was just a baby.

Michael and I traveled up to Philadelphia on the train for some reason; maybe the fleshmobile was broken down. You'd have thought I was taking him on a rocket to Mars; he was so excited. It was his first train trip. I bought him something to snack on, and he sat by the window, shouting out everything he saw. I'm sure it was a long trip for the other people in the railcar.

When we arrived at the station in Philadelphia, my parents were standing on the platform, which floored me. They gave Michael a hero's welcome, as though he was their grandchild and not a complete stranger dragged home by their odd, uncommunicative son. Yet here was my dad, hugging and clowning with this little kid he'd never met, simply because I'd brought him home with me.

I could see Michael's eyes grow wide as we pulled into the driveway of the house in Berwyn. It had so much green grass around, such big flowering shrubs and towering trees. To him, it must have looked like Beverly Hills. My dad kept up his usual little-kid patter the whole way home—playing car bingo and "I Spy" and telling stories in a torrent of good cheer. In retrospect, it seems an act of supreme selfishness, on my part, to bring an eight-year-old stranger to my parents' house and expect them to look after him while I went to work with the Russian landscapers. But hard as my relationship with my parents was, I knew that they would love having Michael invade their space. Luke and I were grown. It had been a while since they had little-boy energy filling up that big house of theirs. Perhaps my dad couldn't deal with a teenager who talked back and had his own ideas about his life, but a boy who hadn't already heard all his jokes and stories? That was heaven.

Was I hesitant about imposing a little kid on my parents? Not at all. Michael was one of God's children. He needed love, and they had plenty to spare. And along the way, Michael could be a great Robin to Dad's daily Batman adventures. Also, you'd have had to be made of stone not to find young Michael Mattocks completely loveable.

Michael, baiting a hook

3. "The Gifts Which We Are About to Receive"

MICHAEL MATTOCKS

My mother got herself a good boyfriend down in Southeast. His real name was Larry, but everybody called him Don. He worked at NASA and made real money. Don was a clean-cut dude, and jolly. Being a janitor and all, he kept his place real nice. Before he and my mom started seeing each other, she'd bring all us kids by his apartment so he could babysit. He would correct us if we were out of line, but he was never mean to us. He used to buy us Christmas, and take us places. We all liked him a lot; he was probably my favorite of my mother's boyfriends.

J.P. was coming around a lot in those days. Sometimes it would be every day. He never stayed around the house with us; the whole point seemed to get us out of the house. Sabrina would go with us sometimes, but usually it was just me and James. I tried to be good all the time with J.P.; I knew he was doing something nice for us, and I didn't want to be no trouble. James, though. Just about every time we'd go someplace, James would end up getting in a fight with somebody. I used to feel bad about that; I mean, bringing that all down on J.P. wasn't fair. J.P. didn't seem to mind too much though. He'd just pull James off whoever it was James was fighting, and right away everything would calm back down. My mom could never do that. She'd break up a fight and then give James a licking, and the whole situation would get louder and more tense.

One day J.P. said he was going to visit his parents in Philadelphia for the weekend and did I want to go. Did I? James didn't come with us; he was sick. J.P. took me to the train station, and there on the platform sat this big-ass shiny silver train. It was hissing and rumbling, and I was about out of my mind with excitement. J.P. bought me a bag of peanuts and let me have the window seat. I couldn't believe how fast that thing went! We were flying! Before I knew it, we were in Philadelphia. "Come on, buddy," J.P. said, standing up as the train slowed down. He always called me "buddy." Then he looked through the window, saw something, and said to himself, "Whoaaaa."

His mom and dad were waiting for us there on the platform. It looked to me like J.P. hadn't expected that and didn't quite know what to make of it. His mom gave him a hug, but it was like he and his dad were in two different worlds; they didn't even look at each other. I could see right away something was a little weird between them. J.P.'s dad, though, he wrapped me up in a big old hug. I hadn't had a man hug me like that since Willie. J.P.'s mom too; she hugged me.

I admit I was a little scared getting in their car and driving off with them. If J.P. hadn't been there, I probably wouldn't have gone. The whole thing was so new and different. All this fuss they were making over a kid; I wasn't used to that. And the big, rich houses out the window were like something out of a movie or a storybook. J.P.'s father seemed to be working awfully hard to make me laugh and keep me calm. He kept up a solid stream of jokes all the way home. I wasn't all that used to men to begin with, especially ones making a lot of effort to be nice to a kid. I admit that until I knew J.P.'s parents better, I felt a little like those kids in the fairy tale who get given lots of candy by the witch to fatten them up for the pot.

And man, their house! It was on this long road with no side-walks, and we turned into a driveway like another whole road. It ended at this big-ass house, standing all by itself and not at-tached to the ones next to it; I hadn't seen too many of those in my life. Trees all around, flowers, big bushes with blossoms on them, and a big dog. I didn't know what I'd gotten myself into.

J.P.'s dad took me through the house, while the big dog fol-lowed us licking me and trying to get me to play. They had lots of Jesus things on the wall, I do remember that. And pictures of J.P. and his brother everywhere. The house went on and on, rooms after rooms. All the furniture matched. Nice rugs. Clean. And quiet—quiet like I'd never heard in Washington. Out the back door was a little swimming pool! J.P. had taken me to pools a couple of times in Washington, but they were indoors, and kind of mossy, and full of people. This one sat out in the sun-shine with the water all sparkly, and it was all for them. Nobody else in it. J.P.'s dad said he'd teach me to swim.

Mrs. P called us in to dinner, but as I started approaching the table, she took me by the shoulders and marched me into a bathroom where she stood over me as I washed my hands. We sat at a table set all nice like in a fancy restaurant, and I reached for a thick slice of bread poking up from a pretty basket with a napkin in it. But J.P. touched me on the arm. His mom had her eyes closed and her head bowed, with her hands folded in front her. "Let us pray," she said, and I folded up my hands like hers and bowed my head, but didn't close my eyes. I wanted to see this shit. J.P. had his hands folded and his eyes closed too. "Bless us, O Lord, and these, Thy gifts, which we are about to receive from Thy bounty. Through Christ, our Lord. Amen." We unfolded our hands, and Mrs. P started handing around food.

I always got enough to eat at home, but man, the meal Mrs. P cooked for us! It was vegetable lasagna; I'll never forget that. Vegetable lasagna! And milk! Mrs. P put a big glass of it in front of me and told me to drink it all up. I didn't drink much milk, usually. We put it on cereal. But something about that milk, all cold, in a real pretty glass, tasted special. I drank it all up, and she poured me another glass. We had salad with lots of things in it I didn't recognize—cucumbers, probably. Radishes. And a cake for dessert. Man!

We played Ping-Pong in their big basement after dinner, and then when it was time for bed, they let me sleep in J.P.'s old room. I wasn't used to sleeping in a room all by myself and was a little freaked out there in the dark, and the quiet. Then came a tapping at the door, and in walked J.P.'s dad. "Hey," he whispered. "Want me to tell you a story?"

"Sure," I said, struggling to sit up.

"No, you stay lying down. Close your eyes. Now this is the story of a little boy who lived in the swamps of Florida back in the last century. And you know what? He had a pet deer. He called his deer Flag because when it ran, its white tail popped up like a flag. Now, this boy . . ." On he went, for what seemed like hours. The boy and his dad killed a big bear, and went hunting, and got lost. Then one day the deer ate the family's garden, and the boy had to tie him up, but he got free and finally came the day that the boy's mother shot the deer. Only she made a mess of it, only hit the deer in the leg, and it ran off, and the boy had to chase after it with a gun and kill it his own self. My eyes started to close because I figured that was the end of the story, but he kept right on going. That boy built himself an airplane and went flying out West where he made friends with lots of animals and formed them up into a little army, and they went around freeing other animals from zoos. . . . Well, at some point I fell asleep. I don't know how long J.P.'s dad sat there telling that story, but it sounded to me like he could have gone all night.

The next morning J.P. went off to work some job. Mr. P drove me into town, and as we were speeding along, he suddenly said, "Hold on!" and the car went over a really big bump. For a second it felt like we were flying. I laughed and laughed, so hard that Mr. P said, "Should we do it again?"

"Yeah!" I shouted, and damned if he didn't stop that car, turn it around and go back over that bump at top speed. And then again. When we got tired of that he took me to a shoe store and said I could have any pair of shoes I liked. I got me some sharp Nikes; my first. Then we had some ice cream. J.P.'s dad was a lot like J.P. He asked me questions all the time: How many brothers and sisters did I have? What did I like doing after school? What's my favorite flavor of ice cream? What's the best part of Saturdays? Did I go to church? I did my best to keep up, but damn, the questions kept coming. He was also like J.P. in that he just took me around no matter what he had going on.

He needed to go see some nuns—I had the impression he did that a lot, just kind of checked in on them—and he took me along. They treated me like a little king, except I didn't like all the cheek-pinching. Then we picked up some dry cleaning and bought groceries, and all the time he was either asking me questions or telling me stories. After a while I started picking up that this dude really liked kids and didn't get to talk to them often enough. That was a trip for me: an older man who liked kids. J.P.'s dad was a trip. He had some kind of job that got him lots of great food that they kept in the freezer in their basement. Mrs. P went down there and brought up all kind of cool stuff: corn dogs, breaded chicken fingers, tubs of barbecue. We had a huge lunch all together, and then Mr. P taught me how to swim.

That day was so warm and sunny and happy. But I remember when J.P. came home, something changed. There was tension between him and his dad that you could feel all over the room. It made me sad. I loved both of those guys so much, and they were so much alike. But for some reason they didn't like each other.

Mrs. P. (in the background), Mr. P., Michael, and David

JOHN PRENDERGAST

As that first summer with the boys was ending, I stumbled into a really good job for a guy interested in urban affairs. Bill Gray was an African-American Baptist preacher from Philadelphia who'd been elected to Congress in 1978. He kept a storefront office at Fifty-Second and Market, a very busy corner in what was at that time a seedy part of West Philadelphia, and for some reason he hired me—the only white guy in the office—to do all-round constituent service while I went to school at Temple University at night.

The office could easily have been the setting for an HBO series, so rich was the cast of characters. Al Smith was a young, smooth, earnest, and ambitious political operative who always wore a perfectly tailored suit and drove a black Corvette; I always felt as though I was in an episode of *Miami Vice* when he and I would go riding around West Philly. Jimmy Simpson was the leader of a local veterans' group, and his empire was built on a hot dog cart in Atlantic City. It seemed Atlantic City only gave hot dog cart licenses to veterans, and while Jimmy had gotten one, he wasn't about to sully his hands actually running it. He had "people" who operated it for him so he could hold court all day at Fifty-Second and Market. Jimmy Smith was a hard-core union organizer with an air for the theatrical who often wore a gleaming white suit; when he walked in, all eyes had to be on him. Frances Walker was the den mother—sturdy, loud, totally committed, and radiant in her mid-forties—she knew everybody's name, everybody's story, everybody's needs. The place was more like a barbershop than a political office. People walked in and out all day, sat around, ate Philly cheese steaks out of waxed-paper wrappings, and talked politics. I spent my day helping constituents—some of the most disadvantaged residents of Philadelphia—cope with everything from Social Security to the Veterans' Administration to getting their water turned back on. "Let Johnny P. handle them old ladies!" Frances would holler. "They love him!"

The job only paid a thousand dollars a month, but I loved

it. I was still in my antimaterialism phase, and the apartment I'd moved into was a $200-a-month rat hole in a dilapidated working-class Italian neighborhood in South Philly. The old ladies sat in front of their houses all day in folding chairs, like sentinels. On the first floor of my house lived a bunch of World War II vets who did nothing all day but drink up their benefits and tell extraordinary war stories extolling their exploits on the battlefield. I lived on the second floor, and on the third was a guy living under a false name because he was running from his child-support payments. My mother was horrified to have her son living in such a place, and she begged me to come home and live with them. I wasn't going to have any part of that, of course. Not so far away from the action, and not with my dad around. Besides, the old Italian ladies loved me—waved and shouted to me every day, made me taste their cooking, and treated me like a long-lost son.

Instead of driving up I-95 every weekend, now I was driving down from Philly to D.C. to see Michael and James. I wouldn't stay in D.C. though; I'd pick up the boys and drive the two or three hours straight back, leave them with my parents, and go off to install shrubbery and mindlessly dig fence post holes—my specialty—with the Russians.

Some summers, my beloved godmother and social justice advocate Aunt Mary arranged for the extended Prendergast family to commandeer what must have been the cheapest rental house on the Jersey shore in a town called Stone Harbor—a big, drafty, pile of splinters that I'd loved since I was a kid. It seemed perfectly natural to bring Michael and James and sometimes even Sabrina to that gathering too, and my aunts and uncles loved having them—especially Uncle Bud and Aunt Jo. Bud was my father's youngest brother, and he had all the Irish storyteller, and all the jokester, that my father had, but little of the dark side that I could see. For a long time I thought it was because he and Jo never had any children.

It wasn't until I was older that Uncle Bud let on what was really up with my father. He took me aside one night down at that shore house, after everyone else had gone to bed, and by candlelight at the kitchen table, he let me in on a family secret. Uncle Bud said that his and my dad's father had a huge personality and was a great storyteller, but he had been mercilessly hard on my dad and at times, had beaten him. I never knew my grandfather. He died the year I was born. But he was a hard-working Irishman of the old school, a steelworker who'd emigrated from Ireland to a rooming house in Youngstown, Ohio, where he and the other Irish mill workers slept in shifts in bunk bed–filled dormitories, and then on to Pittsburgh, where he'd apparently channeled a lifetime of hardship onto his oldest son. By Uncle Bud's account, it was rough, and my dad took it for years.

It was no wonder my dad was a rage-aholic; it was what he'd seen as a child, and it's in some ways remarkable that he was able—to some extent, at least—to limit the violence he wreaked on me to the psychological and emotional. At least now I could start to see a reason why my dad had been the way he was with me. It wasn't an excuse or justification, but it was the beginning of a reason. And the reason had nothing to do with me—with whether I was good or bad. Or unlovable.

Uncle Bud was an open, loving, dynamic guy, and he took a particular liking to James. Something in James' visible psychic wounds really moved that big, florid Irishman. I'd look around for James, and there he'd be, way down the beach digging a sand castle with Uncle Bud. At the big, noisy meals we shared, James would always be tucked up beside Uncle Bud's bulk. I was always grateful to Uncle Bud and Aunt Jo; their special attention to him meant the world to James and to me.

Around this time I decided that since my interest was in the institutions that addressed poverty, I should develop another relationship with a kid like the one I had with Michael and James, but through a proper organization, like Big Brothers Big Sisters, in order to see how such organizations worked. Since Michael and James were in D.C., I figured I'd have the time to take on another kid where I was living in Philly. The man running the Big Brothers Big Sisters office in Philadelphia was named Steve. He was legally blind, very sweet, and caring, and he had a wry, ironic sense of humor. I liked him immediately. We talked for a while—he asked most of the questions—and finally, having heard about my relationship with Michael and James, his face took on a sly smile.

Steve told me he had one boy that was hard to place, named Khayree, who had cancer when he was six and almost died. He even got selected by the Make A Wish Foundation, and they sent him on a last-wish trip to Disney World. He survived, though he lost a leg to the cancer. Apparently no one wanted to be his big brother.

Steve made a phone call, and after a while the door opened. In came an eight-year-old kid. He was wiry and tall for his age, and he was hobbling on a prosthetic leg that seemed as if it had come from Kmart. He didn't have any of Michael's sparkle. Even James, with his instant darkness, was a ray of sunshine compared to this kid. I tried everything with him that I had tried with Michael and James, all the questions—"What's your favorite sport?" "Who's your favorite player?" "What's your favorite movie?" He just looked at me and gave me one-syllable answers. Anybody else probably would have run the other way, but something about this Khayree lit up all my protective tendencies.

He ain't heavy, Father, . . .

I began wrapping Khayree into my schedule. He had a brother, Nasir, who also needed a big brother, so he usually came along when Khayree and I went fishing or out to play. Khayree was a hard kid to reach—much harder than Michael or even James. Losing his leg had really taken it out of him, and he was awash in self-pity. He couldn't say what his favorite sport was because, "I can't play sports." He wouldn't say what games he liked because, "I can't play no games with one leg." He couldn't even tell me his favorite flavor of ice cream. "Don't matter," he muttered, looking down at his prosthetic.

Despite his struggles with self-esteem, I had high hopes for Khayree. He was smart and handsome, and he would flash a radiant smile when he relaxed a bit. I fantasized that maybe he would be a politician or social crusader who could work with me on the issues I cared about when he got older. I would talk his ear off about the injustices of the system and how we might be able to fix them. I was so keen on infusing him with my passions that I didn't try to find out what his were, hidden though they might be.

Khayree loved my dad. Again, at that age, who wouldn't? My dad always had time for him, and he had a way of encouraging him without directly referencing his leg. Khayree found a safe space when he came home with me to my dad and mom's house, and I hoped that could help contribute to the rebuilding of his self-esteem.

I didn't try to keep my new relationship with Khayree a secret from Michael and James, but I didn't bring them together much either. I wanted to keep my relationships with both unique and special, as well as—in retrospect—compartmentalized. I balanced Khayree and Nasir with Michael and James; in one town, one pair of brothers, in another town, the other pair of brothers. And it was all going pretty well for a minute there.

Then I got a call: Steve, the sweet-natured blind man in the Big Brothers Big Sisters office, had walked himself in front of a train. The caller didn't know if it was an accident or not. It hit me hard, not least, probably, because I remembered the night in high school when I almost did the same thing. I wondered about Steve, if he had finally succumbed to being around so much human need, and whether I was placing myself at similar risk. Or was he tortured by his own private demons?

Front row, from left: Rasheed, Luke's wife Kim, Morris, and Khayree. Back row, from left: Tauheed, Luke, Nasir (on Luke's shoulders), and J.P.

That fall, when I was twenty-one, I hurt my ankle playing basketball and couldn't walk for a couple of days. I was sitting in my old recliner chair in my crumbling apartment with my leg up on pillows, icing my ankle, watching a basketball game on television. The set was on a dresser across the room, and if it'd had a remote, I'd have changed the channel or turned the TV off when the game ended. But it was a crummy little black-and-white with a wire hanger for an antenna and no remote, and I couldn't be bothered to roust myself and hop over to change it manually. So I was stuck watching whatever came on after the game. What filled the screen was a news report from Ethiopia, which was then in the midst of a deadly famine that would later trigger the Live Aid concerts and the song, "We Are the World." I was trapped in my recliner chair, staring at the screen, and flabbergasted at what I was seeing—a lunar landscape full of stick-figure children with distended bellies, mothers trying to nurse bony infants, babies with flies on their eyes. It was unfairness on a scale I had never witnessed before.

A spark shot through my memory all the way back to my Spanish teacher, Ms. Kane, and those pamphlets she'd placed on my desk during detention. Remember the scenes in *Close Encounters of the Third Kind* where Richard Dreyfuss has seen Devil's Tower on the television and is inexplicably obsessed with getting there? That's how the images of Ethiopia struck me. I could barely move, my ankle hurt so much, and I had so little money that I was living almost entirely on bowls of Honey Combs and Froot Loops. (Mmmm, Froot Loops.) But I knew I had to get to Africa and understand why this was happening and what we could possibly do about it. My guilt-driven, wanna-be-a-superhero complex kicked in with a roar. I would have hailed a taxi with my crutch to take me to the airport that night if I'd had the money for a ticket.

Now, as educated as I might have been, I was until then

entirely focused on American poverty, and I knew nothing at all about Africa. I couldn't have found Ethiopia on a map. I don't remember if I knew for sure that Africa was a continent and not a country. All I knew was: I had to get there. I called the Ethiopian embassy to ask about visas, and I made the mistake of saying I worked for Congressman Bill Gray. Little did I know, he had sponsored a sanctions resolution against Ethiopia so a visa for one of his staff members was out of the question. The Ethiopian official said I was probably a spy anyway! I studied a map. The next country over from Ethiopia was Sudan, but I was told a U.S. citizen had recently been shot there and the State Department was restricting travel to Sudan for Americans. So I moved my finger across the map to the west and finally settled on Mali.

Mali? Mali had nothing to do with Ethiopia! If I'd been thinking straight, I'd have flown to Kenya, which was closer to the famine and English speaking. It's a measure of my rather unbalanced and completely naive single-mindedness, though, that I fixated on getting to Mali, a French-speaking country whose hunger problems had very little in common with the war and famine in Ethiopia.

I borrowed some money from my parents and threw in what I'd saved, which was enough to buy a one-way ticket to Bamako, Mali's capital. Everybody—from my family to my friends to the people in Congressman Gray's office—thought I was completely off my rocker. Who goes all in to buy a one-way ticket to Bamako?

The next time I saw Michael and James, I told them I was going on a trip to Africa and might not see them for a while. "Africa!" Michael piped. "Lions and tigers?" Lions and tigers, I said. No need to burden him with images of starving babies. I wasn't sure either of them had any idea what Africa was, or how far away. Even the idea of "a couple of months" didn't seem to register with them. After all, they were only eight and six. We went about our day, tearing around the parks of D.C., and forgot all about our coming separation.

My departure for Bamako all happened in a fog; I really had no idea what I was doing or what I was in for. But I was full of confidence because the constant moving since early childhood, though leaving scars, had left me very adaptable, sharpening my social IQ in a Darwinian sort of way.

I changed planes in Paris, but it wasn't for another six or seven hours that the full import of what I had done really struck me. The plane landed in Senegal to refuel in the middle of the night, and everybody got out to have a smoke right next to the plane. I stepped onto the rickety metal staircase to walk down to the tarmac, and the thrilling, mysterious reality of Africa hit me in the nose like a two-by-four. It was roaring hot, and the air was thick with an exotic miasma of dust, diesel, cookfire, and goat. A single, garish light on a pole lit the apron, and palm trees murmured out there in the blackness. Boyish soldiers with enormous guns stood around listlessly. My fellow passengers were drooping with exhaustion, but I felt ready to run a marathon.

As we filed back onto the plane a young, very dark-skinned man in his thirties walked up and introduced himself as Mohammed, working for the Ministry of Agriculture in Mali. "I was at Georgetown with you," he said in a rich, delicately accented voice. "I remember you playing basketball at the field house."

He asked me why I was going to Mali. What could I say? That I'd seen a TV report about the Ethiopian famine, and Mali was as close as I could get? That I had never seen human suffering on that scale and wanted to do something about it? That I was driven by a completely unrealistic, self-aggrandizing mission to help save the world? These answers may have been true, but at that moment I wasn't registering much beyond the simple fact that there were lots of people that needed to be helped, somehow. I don't know exactly what I told him. But I remember his face, and the knowing smile that crossed it. I didn't have to tell him anything, really; he could see I was a naïve, ignorant, well-meaning American kid—which is just about the most unpredictable species on the planet.

If Mohammed hadn't been there to guide me through the Bamako airport, I might still be there. It was utter chaos, a riot of shouting people, soldiers, even livestock. We seemed to pass through half a dozen different formalities—men in ragged uniforms sitting at scarred wooden tables, each wanting a different combination of papers and something else besides. Mohammed argued with every one of them in French or Bambara—two languages it suddenly occurred to me I should have learned before I got on the plane. From his tone he seemed to be saying, "You're not getting anything out of this one, boys; he's with me." Finally we emerged into the raging, smoky sunlight of a Malian morning. Mohammed steered me into a taxi seemingly held together by rust and chicken droppings, and we threaded our way though an updated chapter of the Bible. Robed men and veiled women, donkey carts, goats, listing stucco houses, motorcycles piled with entire families, trucks as old as me belching soot. . . . In my sleepless, mind-blown state, it all passed by the cracked passenger window in an apocalyptic, cinematic, joyous blur.

Mohammed's place was a compound of small clay houses surrounded by a thorn-stick fence on the edge of Bamako. It was a reproduction of three village homes, he told me proudly, but close enough to the center of the city so he could commute daily to work. He shouted into one of the houses, which had no glass in the windows and only a curtain for a door, until a woman emerged holding a bundle of clothing in her arms. "She is my first wife," Mohammed said. "She can move in with one of the others, and you will stay in her house."

"How many wives do you have?"

"Only three. Come."

The walls, ceiling, and floor of the house were made entirely of mud, but the place was immaculate. I had never seen dirt polished so smooth and clean. I had a wooden bed with a colorful cloth thrown over it, and a jug of water on a table. Outside in back was a pit latrine that was as spotless as the house and entirely free of odor. Mohammed told me I was welcome to stay as long as I liked.

I eagerly accepted his invitation to travel with him in his official capacity around the country, inspecting farm projects. I would play with the kids in the various villages we visited and wander in and out of his lengthy meetings with local community groups.

J.P. in Mali, 1984

As we drove, Mohammed behind the wheel of a big gray Land Rover, he talked about the challenges facing African families in putting enough food on their tables. It was a lecture that extended over many weeks and many hundreds of miles, and the gist of it was this:

The global agricultural market, he explained, was entirely geared to give maximum advantage to American and Western European consumers. The World Bank and International Monetary Fund (IMF)—backed by the United States and Europe, their biggest donors—demanded that their client countries, as a condition of receiving loans, divert land from growing locally consumed food to growing the same commodities—cotton, coffee, various grains, and so on—for the sole purpose of creating oversupplies globally that would in turn drive down prices and help keep global inflation at a minimum by producing cheaper food to be sold in our supermarkets and restaurants. In the case of other commodities, massive U.S. government subsidies to Midwestern farmers and a dizzying array of trade barriers allow American agribusinesses to dump cheap products on African and other countries that just can't compete pricewise. Millions of small-scale farmers in developing countries in Africa and elsewhere are impoverished, and their families are needlessly hungry and poor so that Americans and Europeans can pay a penny less for a cup of coffee or a dime less for a t-shirt.

He told this story—in precise, fine-grained, example-backed detail—in a lilting, rolling West African accent entirely devoid of bitterness. Mohammed wasn't blaming me; he wasn't really blaming anybody. To him, this was simply how the world worked. But as I finished my time with him, the implication was clear: Now that I knew all this, what was I going to do about it?

4. Welcome to Somalia

MICHAEL MATTOCKS

Something changed in the life of my mom's boyfriend Don; I was too young to know exactly what. But when I was almost nine years old, he started smoking crack. My mother started drinking with him. There'd be times I'd come in the house and they'd both be in the living room, all fucked up, and skinny little Uncle Artie would be, like, "Gimme that ear," and checking my pockets for change so he could get drunk too.

The summer I turned nine, we moved from Southeast up to North Capitol Street in Northeast D.C. Southeast had been like the country, with the yards and the creek and all, but North Capitol—that was the city. Don and Artie came with us, and two of Aunt Evelyn's kids came too. My mom got a little welfare check every month, and they probably wanted a little piece of that and a place to stay. Somehow we got this big-ass house at 1420 North Capitol, a tall brick townhouse painted gray-blue. Had six bedrooms, which was good, because by then it was Sabrina, me, James, David, Elsie, André, and Tyrell as well as Mom, Don, Aunt Evelyn's two kids, and Uncle Artie.

We moved while J.P. was away in Africa, and I worried he wouldn't be able to find us.

Living on North Capitol Street, man, that was big time. The sidewalk was real wide in front of the house, and North Capitol, shit, it's like six lanes of traffic whizzing by. All that playing in the park and catching crayfish in the stream like we did in Southeast, that was over. We were in the city now for real. We were just a few blocks from Sursum Corda, the baddest housing project in the whole city—maybe the whole country. Man, that motherfucker was tight. I was scared moving up there, I'll tell you the truth. We could see people selling drugs, and hear gunshots at night; you didn't hear that shit in Southeast. One night I'm standing on the corner and see this big flash and hear a loud BOOM about half a block away. A big guy was down in the street with a big hole in his stomach and little pellet marks all around his crotch and thighs. Somebody'd shot him with a sawed-off; I could hear him talking to the ambulance crew. That's the kind of shit went down up there.

We started at a new school, and the other kids teased us because of what we wore. I had three sweat suits—red, black, and blue. I'd mix and match them, but everybody knew that's all I had to wear and ragged my ass about it. The other kids were all wearing Nikes, and me and James were still in these raggedy-assed no-brand-name shoes. I had that pair of Nikes that Mr. P had bought me, but I'd grown out of them by now. James would cry when they teased us, and then he'd go off and get into a big-ass fight and get his ass kicked. Sabrina was off at junior high so she couldn't protect us. It was up to me, and I didn't like that. Like I said, I don't really like to fight. I never did.

Then one day that big ugly tan car pulled up, and there was J.P. My mom had memorized J.P.'s mom's number, and she called and gave her our address, so J.P.'s mom then gave it to

J.P. Me and James piled into the car, and it was like it always was. We went down there on the river behind the Watergate Hotel, bought our little worms from the vending machine, and the whole day slid by. On the way home J.P. spied a big empty parking lot and pulled in there to let me drive his car. Man, I felt like a king behind the wheel of that big car, even if I could barely see over the dashboard. I drove that motherfucker all over that parking lot with James yelling, "Gimme a turn! Gimme a turn!" in the back seat. J.P. didn't let him—James wouldn't have been able to reach the pedals!—and James of course took it as some kind of put-down and threw a complete fit, kicking and screaming and whipping on J.P. with his little arms. There were times I wondered why J.P. kept coming back to us, the shit James put him through.

We always stopped to eat, and that day J.P., as usual, had a big stack of books and papers he brought in with him. Me and James were eating and shooting straw-papers at each other, and J.P. was studying on them books and papers like his life depended on it. It was Africa stuff; I remember lots of pictures of skinny little black children and bony cows.

On the way back to North Capitol, J.P. starting up his questions, like he always did. This time, though, they had an edge to them. "How you doing in school?" he asked me, and I'm sure I said what I usually said, which was, "Fine." Truth was, I hated school. I wasn't the smartest motherfucker in the room, and I was bored all the time, and we had those damned kids putting us down for being shelter kids with no-name shoes. Usually, J.P. would let me leave it at "fine," but this time, he really pressed in. "What do you mean, fine?" he asked. "What grade do you have in math? In social studies?" Like that. I must have giggled, or blown off the question some way, because J.P. got sharp with me in a way he didn't usually do. "I'm not joking around, Michael," he said. "What do you have in math?"

"I don't know," I said. "Probably a D."

"School's important," J.P. said in a kind of scolding voice I'd never heard him use. He sounded disappointed with me all of a sudden, and I didn't know why. "You're not a little kid anymore," he said. "It's time you learned a little accountability. Your mom sends you to school for a reason. School is your job, and doing your work well is what it means to be a man."

"I'm a man!" I said. "Some day I'm going to buy my mom a house!"

"You're not going to buy your mom a house after making D's in fifth-grade math!" J.P. shouted back, really raising his voice.

I didn't know where all this was coming from all of a sudden. For a moment, it flashed on me that J.P. was dying; it was like he was trying to leave me with some last words. Turns out, he wasn't dying, but he was getting ready to check out a little bit. Africa was about to draw him away from us big time, and I think he knew it. On that ride back to North Capitol that day, it felt like J.P. was trying to cram a whole lifetime of being a big brother into fifteen minutes.

We pulled up in front of the big blue-gray house, and I popped the door to get away from him. But he jumped out and came around the car with his arms opened wide. "Hey buddy, come here," he said, and gave me into a big hug. My head only came up to his chest. He held me for a long moment and I let him do it; J.P.'s were the only hugs I got. I think he was apologizing for coming down on me in the car. Or maybe he was saying goodbye.

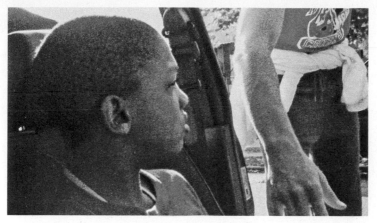

Michael in "the fleshmobile" (with J.P. showing him how to drive)

JOHN PRENDERGAST

After three months in Mali, it was good to get back to my decrepit apartment in the old Italian neighborhood in Philadelphia. The elderly ladies who sat in their aluminum lawn chairs on the sidewalk all day waved and shouted my name as though I was a son returned from the wars. The old vets on the first floor invited me in and tried to get me to have a shot of Canadian Club. Even the mysterious fugitive on the third floor was glad to see me.

It was weird coming back to America, to the abundance and the endless choices. I found myself paralyzed and overwhelmed by the options that a simple grocery store offered. I avoided shopping whenever possible. Bought the same food from the same fast food joints, no longer comfortable going to nicer restaurants or even to large supermarkets. I stopped buying new clothes, getting what I absolutely needed during occasional thrift store visits in South Philly. I stopped using air-conditioning and any other creature comfort. This austerity lasted for years. My only escape from the self-denial was going to the movies, sometimes with my little brothers but often alone, where I would spend hours, buying a ticket and then sneaking into another one or two for a double or triple feature.

Congressman Gray let me come back to my old job in West Philly—helping constituents get their SSI checks, their veterans' benefits, their subsidized rents. I could still summon the old interest in American urban poverty, but something fundamental had changed. I remember helping one old man trying to sort out his troubles with the VA. He had worked at one company nearly his entire adult life and was living all alone on Social Security and a tiny pension, and he had a number of health problems. He had nobody, and no skills for navigating the enormous federal bureaucracy—a very deserving constituent, and just the type of citizen that I'd launched a career to try to help. But as we sat there, knee to knee, in his humble little kitchen, I couldn't help thinking: He eats every day. He doesn't have to walk farther than the tap to get all the fresh water he wants. He has a roof over his head. He doesn't have to worry about starvation, war, and village burnings. And he lives in a country with a reasonably functional bureaucracy and impartial courts, at least in principle. Compared to the people I'd just spent a few months among, he seemed fortunate.

How could the United States, with all its abundance and opportunity, do so little for those people I had seen in the Saharan Desert communities who were fighting a daily battle with hunger and thirst? *The United States has to do more!* Sorting out the terrible injustices inflicted upon people affected by deadly wars and unfair global food markets now seemed the most important thing in the world to me. And until that happened, getting more aid to Africa became an absolute obsession. Food! Medicine! Clothing! Tools! Money! I knew there existed an apparatus to deliver aid to developing countries, but I didn't know anything about it.

I found myself confused. This old man and the others I was assisting in West Philly were no less deserving of help than they were before my trip. But were they the people *I* most wanted to help? I was no longer sure. Now I hungered to figure out the bureaucracy of foreign aid the way I'd once yearned to understand the way services were delivered to poor folks in America. My grazing, nomadic brain was getting ready to run me full speed down an entirely new path.

The most important thing to me was getting back to Africa as quickly as possible. Its pull was so strong that I sometimes felt that a big rusty hook had been embedded under my sternum and was dragging me forward. I began going through the District of Columbia telephone book, looking for any organization with the word "Africa" in its title, hoping to find one that might sponsor my return trip. I finally came upon a group called Operation Crossroads Africa, which organized trips for young Americans to do service work in Africa. I signed on without even asking where they'd send me or what I'd have to do when I was there. All I knew was, it was a way to get back to the continent.

The time I'd spent in Mali was the longest I'd been away from Michael and James since I'd met them. When I returned from this first trip to Africa, I didn't bring them presents because I had no money to buy anything in the places I'd visited. And it wasn't like they were expecting anything; nobody in their family had ever traveled overseas, let alone brought home souvenirs. The same was true for Khayree and Nasir.

What they wanted was me, and I had this deep foreboding in my heart that they were going to get less and less of me in the months and years to come. Africa was drawing me away. I knew it then. It wasn't anything I could explain to them either. We had no frame of reference. I thought that trying to describe what I'd seen in Mali, and how I thought I might be able to make a difference, wouldn't have made much sense, since I was just trying to understand it myself.

It was a serious problem looming before me: the conflict between my growing responsibility to Michael and James, as well as Khayree and Nasir, and my newfound mission to help tackle the unfairness I had encountered in Africa. The old superhero complex was taking over, enveloping me in its spidey web of self-delusion. I believed I could do anything and everything. So naturally, when I'd begin to feel the prickling of a very realistic sense that my work in Africa was going to change my relationship with the boys, I wrapped it up in unrealistic optimism and shoved it under the rug. Of course my newfound interest in Africa wouldn't change my relationship with my little brothers. I could do anything; I could work on causes in Africa *and* remain as present and important in the lives of these little boys as ever. Right?

What came out of my mouth, though, was a kind of desperation to have as much effect on the boys as I could during my weekend visits to Michael and James in D.C. in the little time that I thought I had left with them. Until then, our whole relationship had been built around play. I'd let them lead. You want to go fishing? We'll go fishing. You want to go to the park? We'll go to the park. I was just a big playmate, giving them a break from the grim circumstances in which they lived to have a little fun. To the extent that I was trying to "change" them, it was passive, as a role model. And there was something a little cookie cutter about it all. Everyone got the same inquiries. To a lesser extent, the same was true of Khayree and Nasir too. Firing a bunch of questions gives the interviewer all the control, and doesn't leave much room for sharing. The responder is vulnerable, opening up, believing there's interest, while the interviewer may not be fully listening or diagnosing, dissecting, and determining his or her subject. I was definitely giving them a break, but maybe playing was all I could handle. Perhaps I was modeling my father in a way I wouldn't have acknowledged or even imagined back then.

Now, though, I felt a compulsion to cram into our relationship a new, more active role for myself. I no longer had the leisure to wait for them to acquire my drive and middle-class values by osmosis. If I were going to have the lasting effect on these boys that I wanted to have, I needed to be more direct about it.

At least that's what I thought. As soon as I tried it, though, I could tell the boys didn't like it, and it introduced a new adversarial note into our relationship that didn't do it any good.

I didn't have long to think about it because after a few visits to see the boys in D.C., I had to leave again for Africa with the young do-gooders and adventurers. I suddenly found myself with a group of young Americans in Zanzibar in the middle of the Indian Ocean, which is where the organization rather randomly assigned me to go. Zanzibar has many unique qualities. It is an idyllic tropical island off the coast of mainland Tanzania, heavily scented with the cloves that are its main export (in the region's saddest chapter, slavery was an earlier export "industry"). It has been a regional trading hub from at least the

time of the fall of the Roman Empire, welcoming merchants
from lands as far away as the Arabian Peninsula. The main city
is a delightfully colorful warren of shoulder-width whitewashed
streets, open-air markets, and street vendors selling chunks of
smoked octopus and crispy-hot samosas. It is a fascinating, sen-
sual place to visit with picturesque beaches and a complex history, and the students I was with were smitten. I, of course, was
in no mood for fun in the sun; I was on the trail of the world's
greatest injustices.

Our assignment was to help build a school—a kind of Habi-
tat for Humanity project ten thousand miles from home. It was
a good group of young people, serious about their work, but I
couldn't help noting the irony of importing Americans, at great
expense, to do manual labor in Africa. After all, one thing Africa
has in abundance is people. I liked hanging around some of the
international aid agencies, watching how aid really ended up on
the ground in Africa. Each office had a dear elderly lady whose
sole function seemed to be to fetch tea. Some had very savvy
Zanzibari field employees actually implementing the projects

J.P. with kids in Zanzibar, 1985

gee camp? War? Famine? I put my papers on the patio
up. I wanted to know everything. How did these wars
the people, what were the medical effects of malnutrition,
politics that were driving them across the border, the or-
nizations that were assisting them, the diseases the refugees
ntracted, the types of wounds they suffered from. The poor
woman barely had time to finish one question before, in my
typical fashion, I was firing another at her. She'd been to the very
places I wanted to understand and illuminate. We moved from
the pool to the restaurant, where I grilled her without stop, and
then to her room. Truth be told, I'd have been hard pressed to
tell you which part of the night I enjoyed more, the parts when
we weren't talking or the parts when we were. I crept out of the
room at first light, and went walking downtown to find a travel
agent. I traded in my tourist trip ticket to Mount Kilimanjaro
for a flight to Somalia. One way.

Somalia's main airport was a rerun of Mali's, but now at least
I knew what to expect, and I made it through unscathed. Most
everyone at the airport was trying to get out of the country, not
get in, so I had little competition. And hardly anybody was trying to fly from Mogadishu, the capital, to Hargeysa in the north
of the country, so that was easy too. The people running the
UNHCR camp near Hargeysa were so glad to have another pair
of energetic hands that they barely asked me who I was or how
I'd gotten there, and they accepted me as a volunteer on the
basis of a sole recommendation from the lovely lady back at the
swimming pool in Nairobi. A harried French doctor showed me
to a tent full of sweat-stained cots, pointed to an empty one, and
said, "You can sleep here." A nurse asked if I was hungry and
put in my hands a tin bowl full of what looked and tasted like
Elmer's glue. I was in it now, for real.

around the island. I occasion.
some of these aid workers to se.
here, a fish farm there. . . . There we.
seemed like little raindrops in an ocean.

It was only my second trip to Africa,
already taking a hit. The industrialized wo.
Africa, and from where I stood, it looked to
the United States, we weren't willing to address
inequalities that were causing deep poverty in Afric
demand for cheap food and raw materials and our lac.
tained commitment to investing in peace and democracy.

At the end of our stay in Zanzibar, the students and I h
to Nairobi. They were all heading off for a couple of weeks to
the Ngorogoro Crater, Mount Kilimanjaro, and the other great
tourist attractions of East Africa—a trip I had little interest in.
Most of them were hanging out in the bar, enjoying their first
beers in weeks, so I took advantage of a few hours off and wandered out to the hotel pool with a stack of reports and position
papers to keep me company. The news out of Ethiopia was staggering: deaths by the thousands.

A shadow fell across the papers. "You heading up there?" an
American voice said. I looked up to find a very attractive young
blonde woman standing over me.

She told me she worked for the UN refugee agency in Hargeysa, northwest Somalia. Near the Red Sea and east of the
Ethiopian border. The United Nations' High Commissioner for
Refugees (UNHCR) and a bunch of NGOs had camps there
for Ethiopians who had fled the war and famine in the Oga-
den Desert. She was taking a few days to decompress, which she
needed because of the intensity of the situation there.

Someone handed me a clipboard and sent me over to a fenced compound full of trucks. *Keep track of the food coming in,* were my instructions, *and make sure it gets sent to the parts of the camp that need it.* Young Somali men were heaving white sacks off the trucks and stacking them into neat mountains. The heat was unbelievable. The papers on the clipboard told me how many sacks of grain the men were unloading. When I counted the bags, though, about a third of them were missing.

"Welcome to Somalia," a wiry, bearded Australian told me when I checked with him about it. He told me how the Somali president, Siyaad Barre, had his henchmen take their cut of the food aid right at the Red Sea port, adding that other soldiers would take further slices as the food made its way to the refugees.

He pointed out that Siyaad Barre was one of America's most reliable Cold War allies in Africa. "What's your expression? 'He's a bastard, but he's *our* bastard?' Killing his own people, and stealing from the ones he doesn't kill. Your tax dollars in action, mate." The Australian laughed and walked away.

I stayed in the refugee camp for a few months, and here is a partial list of what I learned: War can reduce people to abject deprivation and family dislocation faster than anything else in the world; the brains of malnourished children weigh less than those of kids who eat properly; a bullet fired from an AK-47 will tumble around in the human body, causing horrific wounds; foreign aid can be a real money-maker for unscrupulous officials; kwashiorkor is a deficiency of protein, whereas marasmus is a deficiency of both protein and calories; the United States gives food aid not only to keep people alive but also to prop up grain prices for U.S. farmers; land mines can look like little toys and often lure children to them; the diseases that ravage the people of Africa include schistosomiasis, river blindness, sleeping sickness, Guinea worm infection, a hundred varieties of dysentery, tuberculosis, polio, cerebrospinal meningitis, and malaria.

Most important, I learned that geopolitics, not compassion, were driving American foreign policy, which meant that real problem solving was rarely a priority. In Somalia, for example, the United States was willing to provide money and munitions to a thieving, murderous dictator like Siyaad Barre because he was nominally a counterweight to Soviet influence in Ethiopia on the Cold War chessboard of the 1980s. He was killing, torturing, imprisoning, and starving his own people, and U.S. taxpayers were unwittingly underwriting much of the mayhem.

My stay in the refugee camp in Somalia shifted my entire perspective on what the solution should be. Until then, I'd thought the solution was more generous amounts of foreign food and medical aid. Now I was learning that the policies of countries like the United States in the context of the Cold War helped prop up dictators and actually promoted conflict. Sending more aid just treated the symptoms. Sure, the aid kept people alive, which was crucial, but they could be killed the next day by ammunition subsidized by American taxpayers in tandem with the food aid we were sending. Mind-bending lessons for a foreign policy novice.

What followed was the very question that Mohammed had left me with in Mali: Now that I knew how my own country was part of the problem, what would I do with that knowledge? How could I help change America's policies to stop making matters worse in Africa? And now that I'd seen the effects of war in that refugee camp, shouldn't I do more to promote peace? So what should I do next? Do I work my way up to running one of these humanitarian aid agencies? Do I sign on for a life of refugee camp work, bathed in righteous sweat but feeling overwhelmed by the bottomless need all around me? Do I walk away from the whole thing as too complex for my pure intentions? And if so, would I just turn my back on the people whose lives had been torn apart by war and whose plight had stirred me to action in the first place?

No chance I walk away. I wanted to dig deeper and get at the root causes of these crises. And then dedicate my life to figuring out how to get my own government to stop being part of the problem and start becoming part of the solution.

The trip to the refugee camp in Somalia brought about the dawning of a realization that took me by surprise: It wasn't going to be enough to visit every conflict-torn corner of Africa and understand each famine and war firsthand. I was going to have to work the other side of the ocean. I was going to have to become equally expert in the politics of foreign policy in Washington, D.C. If I was going to be as effective as I wanted to be at changing the way the world protected its most vulnerable, I was going to have to become as comfortable in a jacket and tie as I was in sweat-stained khakis.

And since I had given away all my jackets and ties, I thought that might pose a problem.

I didn't have much time to think about all of this because as soon as I got back to the United States, I learned that a runaway train was heading right at Michael and his family, and they didn't even know it was coming.

5. "Earn It Myself"

MICHAEL MATTOCKS

James and I spent a year on North Capitol knocked back on
our heels a little bit—scared of the violence around us and
put down by the kids in school—before I started figuring
out that what I had to do was make some money to buy us
some motherfucking clothes. That's how it started with me;
I was sick of me and my little brother getting dissed for what
we wore. I was eleven by then; starting to become a man. And
there was this dude hanging around because he liked my sister, Sabrina, who could teach me the ways of the life. His name
was Gomez.

Gomez was about fourteen. He lived with his mom, Miss
Lucille, and his stepdad Ellis, and was polite the way you'd expect of a guy living with two parents. He was a clean-cut dude.
Dark-skinned. Built. He used to wear a sweat suit everywhere,
had a little gold on, and always had money in his pocket. It took
me a while to figure it out, but eventually I did: Gomez was a
drug dealer.

He was the first drug dealer I had ever hung out with. I
remember thinking: I want to be just like this motherfucker.
He's got the rings, he's got the clothes, he's got the moves. He

ain't scared up here; he's living it! Even though it was my big sister he was interested in, it was me who hung around him. I stuck by Gomez as much as I could, watching how he did the thing—how he'd get himself a ball of crack about the size of a baseball, cut it up with a knife into little nuggets the size and color of teeth, slip the nuggets into plastic bags no bigger than a postage stamp, and sell them on the street. He made it look so easy, like there were no cops to worry about or nothing.

I watched how Gomez got by until one day I cut off some chunks of Ivory soap into little pieces and sold them for $20 apiece. Before I knew it, I had a couple hundred dollars in my pocket! Eleven years old! I took that money, and James and me went right out and got us some real Nike shoes, just like Mr. P had bought me.

I cut up some more soap and ran off to another block to sell it. I didn't worry about some crackhead coming back and kicking my ass. By the time they come back, you ain't around anymore. And even if they see you, it's too late. The money's gone. And anyway, they're crackheads. I was already learning that most of the time they don't do shit.

Right around then, though, a guy in the neighborhood got killed passing off bits of soap as crack. Crackhead came back and shot him six times in the head; dumped him in the trash can. That word went around North Capitol like a fucking wildfire, and I knew right then I had to straighten my shit out or get out of the game altogether. I wasn't ready to give it up. I liked buying things for my brothers and sisters. I liked bringing home a little money for my mom. She and Don were drinking pretty bad by then and were fucked up most of the time. If I wanted to have money in my pocket, I was going to have to earn it myself. But I sure as hell didn't want to end up in no trash can with six bullets in my head.

I used to climb out the third-floor window of my house at night after my mom would go to sleep. I'd stay out until the sun came up with my buddies: Albert, Mickey, and one kid who became real important in my life, Little Charles. Little Charles was my age—eleven—but he seemed older because he really knew the streets. He wasn't anybody to be afraid of; he was short and skinny, with dark brown skin. But he walked around those nasty streets at all hours like he owned them, because he was smart. He observed things. One of the tricks he taught me was to melt a candle in a pot and mix in some baking soda and a tube of Orajel when it's all bubbling. Crackhead's liable to bite a little piece before he buys; the baking soda gives it that chalky quality, and the Orajel makes his tongue numb, just like crack. Sell that, move on to the next block. Little Charles walked with me, and he knew who to sell to and who not to fuck with. "Not that guy," he'd say. "He'll whip your ass. That one over there. He'll buy." Little Charles could be a crazy-ass motherfucker too. One night he and I smashed the back window of a Jeep Cherokee, stuck a snatch bar in the ignition, and peeled out. We were joyriding like a motherfucker when a police car fell in behind us. I figure we're caught sure, but Little Charles stomps the gas and off we go. Those cops chased us all over Northeast but never caught us. Little Charles finally gave them the slip. That's why I've always liked Jeep Cherokees since then; I know they can go.

I'll tell you what: Little Charles was my best friend, no doubt about it.

JOHN PRENDERGAST

As soon as I got home from Africa, I spoke to one of the social workers familiar with Michael's family's case. She told me that given the litany of family problems, Denise could be heading toward a situation in which she would be at risk of losing the kids to foster care. I decided to ask Denise if I could take Sabrina, Michael, and James—the three oldest—off her hands for the summer and have them come live with me in Philly. This could potentially relieve some of the pressure on her, allow her to focus on her four younger kids, and maybe get some help for her own problems.

Denise agreed to let me take them for a while. I said I'd check in with her in a few days, and I took the kids with me out to my car. We shot north on I-95 and were back in Philly in two and a half hours.

I wasn't prepared for the reaction in my little Italian neighborhood. Instead of waving me over to give me a hug, the old ladies on the street pulled themselves arthritically out of their aluminum lawn chairs, turned them 180 degrees, and sat back down with their backs to me. The old vets on the first floor pushed their door closed from the inside when they saw me in the hall. Mine happened to be one of the blocks in the neighborhood that hadn't yet been "broken," as some realtors called it back then, meaning inhabited by black families, which in that perverse, corrupted system, drove housing prices down dramatically. The sight of three little black kids coming and going from my apartment was the harbinger of doom for them, as they saw it. Hardly anyone in the neighborhood ever spoke to me again after Michael, James, and Sabrina moved in.

I didn't have beds for them—I didn't even have enough chairs for us all to sit around a table together—but none of that mattered to the kids. One of 'em kept peeing on the cushions they slept on, but I'm not saying who. Once they fought over who would sleep where; suffice it to say Sabrina won. It was all a big adventure to them.

I had graduated from Temple University by then, my fifth college in my cross-country wanderings, and I was taking graduate courses at the University of Pennsylvania. I was still working in Congressman Gray's office, and on weekends I'd go work with the Russian landscapers. As soon as I knew the kids were going to stay with me for the summer, I sent out word to all my friends, my brother Luke, and my parents: All hands on deck. My old Georgetown roommate Geoff came to Philly and stayed with us for a while to help me out, and those kids really took to him. He is one of the greatest spinners of fantastic yarns I've ever met. In my dad's league on that one. The kids were mesmerized by his tales and his flashy car, gold chain, stylish clothes, and smooth dance moves, and he and the kids would break-dance for hours to Michael Jackson songs.

Basic nutrition for the kids was not an insignificant challenge. Friends and family would bring casseroles over, and I had just enough knowledge of the kitchen to be able to heat them up. Otherwise, we ate a lot of Honey Combs. And hot dogs—I knew how to boil them, a dozen at a time. Once I tried to cook a chicken; the desiccated piece of plastic that emerged from the oven brought an unceremonious end to my culinary career before it began.

Of course, there was my parents' house as a fallback, and we spent a lot of days and nights over there. By now the novelty of the kids had worn off, and my parents treated them like their own. Wash your hands. Grace before supper. Sit up straight. Weed the flower bed. Skim the leaves off the pool. My parents cleaned them up every Sunday and took them to church. It was great for everybody; my parents got a chance to act like parents again, and the kids got the kind of structure and rigorous love they needed.

Sabrina, Michael, and James were with me for the whole summer. I couldn't leave them alone in the apartment, so I took them with me everywhere. At first, the people in Congressman Gray's office didn't know quite what to make of that. It didn't take long, though, for them to figure it out. Of course, everybody in the office loved those kids. They'd ply them with candy and make up little games for them, give them scratch paper to draw pictures on, even dream up little jobs for them—sorting buttons, cleaning out desk drawers—just to see them go at it so eagerly. I could go off in the fleshmobile to help some old lady sort out her electricity bill or fight with her landlord, and I knew the kids would be perfectly well cared for until I got back.

That was my way: I made the kids everybody's responsibility. There was a gym not far from my house where I liked to play basketball and lift weights. I'd take the kids there and let them run around while I worked out. I figured someone would look after them, and someone always did. They'd get into a game, or hang out by the snack bar getting people to buy them treats, or amuse themselves with the medicine balls. Half the time there'd be some disaster—they knocked over a rack of free weights, they left the water running in the bathroom and flooded the place—and I'd have to deal with that. But there wasn't any other choice. I'd made them mine for the summer, but I wasn't going to give up my life. I simply counted on the goodwill of those around me.

I was still trying to keep my relationship with Khayree and Nasir alive too, but even someone as socially clueless as I could tell that trying to bring the two families of kids together wasn't a good idea. I tried it a couple of times, but they didn't click. Khayree was too withdrawn, and Nasir too young and volatile. James invariably would find something to feel offended about and go off on one of his violent rages. Michael and Sabrina were decent and open to Khayree and Nasir, but they didn't really connect with them.

All this time, I was sending letters to organizations in Washington, D.C., trying to find a job that would take me back to issues like the Ethiopian famine, which had sparked my interest in Africa in the first place. Finally, I got a letter from an organization called Bread for the World—one of the groups, coincidentally, that had produced some of the pamphlets my Spanish teacher Ms. Kane had showed me back in high school—offering me a position as an intern with a yearly stipend of $8,000. Perfect.

It meant, though, that I had to move back to Washington. I couldn't just drop Khayree and Nasir, of course, so I leaned hard on my brother Luke to fill in for me. Luke had internalized our upbringing—and the "he ain't heavy" ethic of Boys' Town—his own way: He'd become a teacher at a high school in inner-city Philadelphia. It was perpetually hard work but incredibly rewarding because of the socioeconomic circumstances of the students, and it required a level of commitment to young people—a day-to-day, minute-to-minute commitment, sustained over years—that I couldn't fathom. I was such a nomad, endlessly moving from one engagement to the next. Michael, James, and their family were the only exception to that rule, and even that was hard for me to sustain. Luke went deep. He'd grown into a big, handsome man with a biting and understated wit, whose sad, heavily shadowed eyes revealed the depth of his empathy for the suffering of others, an empathy that was much quieter than mine. I admired him tremendously, but that didn't keep me from demanding that he pick up the pieces in my wake.

I wheedled from Luke a promise to "take over" my relationship with Khayree and Nasir, to slip into my shoes as big brother. As soon as Luke mumbled his assent—what else could he do?—I was off like a shot. I loaded Michael, James, and Sabrina into the fleshmobile along with my favorite Archie Bunker chair, reading lamp, books, and clothes and raced down I-95 as fast as I could. I pulled up in front of the big blue-gray house on North Capitol and let the kids out.

It was a little nerve-wracking to be back there again. Up on North Capitol, drug dealers openly hung out on the sidewalks, giving passers-by the stare down. Sursum Corda, the roughest housing project in the District, lay barely a quarter mile away, and the sounds of sirens from over there were constant, peppered with occasional gunshots. *Luckily*, I thought, *the boys are too young to get in any kind of serious trouble*; Michael wasn't but twelve years old, and James ten. What worried me most was that North Capitol Street was a huge boulevard, with cars whizzing by at forty miles an hour. I could picture one of the kids running out into the street after a bouncing ball and getting smashed. I was more worried about that in my self-protective state of ignorance than of the real dangers and temptations that the boys faced on a daily basis.

But the good news was that my social worker contact told me that any talk of taking the kids away from Denise had dissipated, and Denise herself felt a bit renewed from the break she had gotten. I'm not sure the family ever even knew how close they had come to being broken up and the kids thrown into the foster care system. That train wreck was averted, but other disasters were in formation.

As though I didn't have enough going on, between the new job and the boys, I enrolled in a graduate program at American University, after attending a semester of graduate school at the University of Pennsylvania, where I accumulated a few lackluster Cs and one lifetime friend, Adam Braufman, who used to sit in the back of class with me and pass notes back and forth about our dreams beyond those academic walls, as well as our endless Sixers versus Celtics debates. So American U. was lucky college number seven. Lord knows I didn't want to leave myself a spare minute. I might have relaxed. I might have had a girlfriend. I might have slept more than four to five hours a night. But I guess self-declared superheroes don't have steady girlfriends. Comic book heroes don't sleep.

J.P. and James

Michael, Sabrina, and Mr. P.

6. The Unthinkable

MICHAEL MATTOCKS

It felt good to get back to North Capitol, to tell the truth. The summer in Philadelphia with J.P. was fun—getting to know all those new people, hanging with Mr. and Mrs. P in their big house—but I'd gotten a little taste of that fast nighttime life back in D.C., and I kind of missed it. Soon as I returned, I went back to cooking up my phony crack out of soap, baking powder, and Orajel. I hid what I was doing from James and Sabrina. Sabrina would have kicked my ass, and James, he wasn't but about ten years old then. I was going to sixth grade and all, but on the lunch break I'd go out to the corner and sell my shit. Miss Hurston would come out and say, "What you doing?" I think she knew, but what was she going to do about it? Put me out of school? She knew I'd have liked that; I could be out on the corner all damn day.

Selling bits of soap and candle, though, you make kid money. Candy-bar-and-sneakers money. Pretty soon I wanted to be in the life full time. James and I had a job pumping gas, and I'd watch the drug dealers come in and out in their nice rides, thinking, *That's what I want.* I was the oldest, and I felt like I was the man of the house. I wanted to take care of my family, and this was the best way to do it.

One day a dealer comes in driving a big-ass Cadillac, and when I open the gas cap, a little bag of rocks falls out. I look up; the dealer is busy talking to somebody, and I think, *Should I put this in my pocket?* I chickened out, though, and handed it to him. He laughed and gave me $30.

Just holding those crack rocks in my hand that one minute, though, helped me make up my mind. One day I asked Gomez to get me some of the real thing. He came by the house and took from his pocket a handful of tiny little plastic bags, each one with a tiny white nugget in it—my first real crack cocaine. I held it in my hand, and it seemed to pulse with power—like holding a little bit of uranium or some radioactive shit. Something way more powerful than it looks. I could see with my own eyes what that shit was doing up and down the block. I could see people so burned up by crack that they looked like scarecrows. But I could also see how fine the people who were selling it were dressed, and how tall they walked. I gave Gomez the $100 I had saved, and he gave me twenty-five of those little bags; told me to charge $25 apiece for them. When Sabrina and my mom weren't paying any attention, I went out there on the street and offered them up. Little Charles took me by the hand and showed me how to get it done, but really, it was like pouring water on the ground in the middle of the desert. Those twenty-five were gone in a single heartbeat, and I had $500 in my pocket. $500! For about a half-hour's work!

Things started to get really crazy for me up on North Capitol Street. I saw people getting shot, getting beat up. I started getting used to the violence, to the dope fiends that used to scare me so much.

I started hanging around with some older guys, and some of

them were real killers. The truth is I was attracted to the power those dudes had. No one ever fucked with them, and everyone respected them. I wanted that. I was tired of getting picked on for wearing those three sweat suits and being called dirty. That shit had to end.

But I had to do things to earn that respect for myself. It got easier and easier for me to do some of the things that I used to be scared of. As soon as I could afford some better clothes, I would go to school with a .22 in my pocket that Little Charles lent to me. Everything changed. The older guys started looking out for me. After that, nobody picked on me or none of my brothers and sisters.

JOHN PRENDERGAST

Around this time, money was tight for me. Getting rich was never part of the justice advocate's plan, but dancing on the poverty line wasn't either. To make ends meet, I sold my beloved baseball card collection, which was probably bringing me bad karma anyway because Luke and I had shoplifted so much of it—one pack or box of packs at a time—from grocery and drugstores in all the places we were growing up. Then the basketball card collection. Then football. Even the booklet of player stamps that my dad had helped me collect from gas stations when I was seven—every player in the NFL. Then my treasured comic books, when things got really tough.

To save rent money, I moved into—or more accurately, squatted in—a sparse unit in a condemned apartment building about ten blocks east of where the boys were living. Even by the standards of the places to which I'd become accustomed, it was on the edge. People were always prowling around on the back porch of the house at night, and because of the position of one of the streetlights, their shadows would be projected on my bedroom wall in eerie detail. Water and power had long been switched off by the utility companies, but somebody had jury-rigged them back on. The only problem was, the two systems had somehow gotten scrambled, and whenever I took a shower, I'd get a tiny electric shock about every thirty seconds—a constant reminder of my squatter status.

Bread for the World was engaged in exactly the sort of work I'd hoped to learn: moving American public opinion toward effective policies to combat hunger both in the United States and abroad. This was the mid to late 1980s, and conservative Christian organizations were getting a lot of attention and praise for organizing church members all over the country into political constituencies against abortion rights and gay rights, and in favor of things like vouchers for religious schools. Bread for the World, which took its name from the edict enunciated in the Book of Matthew—"I was hungry and you gave me bread"—aimed to marshal a similar faith-based constituency in the fight against world hunger. When I joined, it was trying to found a chapter in every congressional district, in the hopes of elevating the fight against world hunger to an urgent issue for Christians, and one that they would take action to rectify.

It was an uphill fight. The Cold War was still the overriding organizing principle of American foreign policy, and the United States did little overseas that didn't somehow give it a millimeter of advantage over the Soviet Union. The loudest Christian voices called themselves the Moral Majority at the time. I never believed they were a majority. They certainly weren't focused on poverty, and they were zealous supporters of budget cuts for poor people's programs. One prominent official proclaimed, "Let them eat cheese," referring to the government's surplus cheese distribution programs, which did more for subsidized dairy farmers than for poor children's nutritional status, and the government at the time tried to get ketchup certified as a vegetable for the school lunch program in order to save money.

Bread for the World had one small advantage though. It had been founded by Art Simon, the brother of Illinois Senator Paul Simon, who was new to the Senate then and in a position to ask his colleagues to at least see activists from Bread for the World. Nominally, I worked out of an old warehouse at Eighth and Rhode Island Avenue in Northeast D.C. where Bread for the World kept its headquarters. My job, though, was on Capitol Hill, walking the halls of Congress and trying to buttonhole staffers. I'd harangue them about hunger in places like Somalia and Ethiopia and about the need for the United States to invest in solutions. It became clear to me the first week that few on Capitol Hill knew much about what was really happening in the most forgotten corners of the world. The geography of my beat—the Horn of Africa, Congo, Rwanda, Liberia, Zimbabwe, and so on—obviously meant little to them.

At first I was depressed at the general lack of knowledge, but then slowly I began to see opportunity. There was no real opposition to alleviating hunger or to making peace; the obstacles were ignorance and apathy. Somebody who really understood the issues, and who also knew how Washington worked, could nudge the ship of state in the proper direction. Heck, the staff

members were so overworked that they were happy to have people like me help them draft legislative language.

I was seeing the boys a lot during this period. We'd still go
fishing and play in the park, but mostly our time together was
jammed with my job. Just as I had done when working for Congressman Gray in Philadelphia, I brought the boys to work with
me, and I counted on both their good behavior and other people's goodwill to make it work. My friend Mike Bandstra and I
would sit up on the roof of the Bread for the World warehouse,
which overlooked Washington, D.C.'s dual face of majesty and
destitution, and argue politics while the boys ran around playing hide-and-seek or football. Luckily for me, Bread for the
World had hired a gorgeous young intern named Melissa Day
who really loved Michael and James and spent hours with them.
Melissa knew how to talk to them in a way that drew out long
conversations. I'd be on the phone, or studying some report on
my desk, and I'd glance over to see Michael and James talking
on and on with Melissa. She also hugged them a lot, and they
couldn't get enough of that.

I had some vague sense that bringing the boys with me to
work would expose them to the functioning professional world
and give them aspirations beyond the petty crime and the various other negative influences they were exposed to every day.
But that was mostly just an excuse. I brought them to work with
me because I wanted to be working all the time. I didn't really
want to burn an entire day fishing anymore. In a single day, a
thousand African children might die; how could I spend that
day casting for catfish in the Potomac? The options for me were
either bring the boys to work or not see the boys at all, and I
couldn't have that.

But I was increasingly only half there for them. One night during a visit to Philadelphia, the boys and I were driving around with my brother, Luke, and it was very hot—one of those humid, leaden nights that made everybody cranky. We all needed to get out of the car, and we stopped near the Art Museum, at one of the big, ornate fountains in downtown Philly. We couldn't help splashing each other, it was so hot, and before I knew it, the kids were in the fountain, fully clothed, up to their knees. I knew I should have scolded them and pulled them out, but they were so lit up with glee that I couldn't bring myself to do it. Before I knew it, Luke was in there with them, splashing and yelling and hamming it up. I thought about climbing in myself, but then I remembered that I hadn't yet read a report on Africa from the United Nations that had just been released. I had an appointment the following afternoon with Congressman Mickey Leland back in D.C., and I wanted to be fully prepared. So while Luke and the kids played, I sat under a street lamp and pored through the report.

That image—the boys scraped off onto Luke momentarily so I could cram in another hour of work on Africa—is emblematic of my relationships. I'd never fully been a brother to Luke. I'd been willing to use him as a buffer against Dad, but I'd never really brought him into my heart the way a big brother ought to. And now I was using him again, just the way I was using my parents as caregivers for the boys without acknowledging any appreciation for my dad's efforts.

Even so, the boys had bestowed upon me another chance at childhood. They were helping me understand my father in terms of the challenges of dealing with kids with independent or even rebellious natures, and they were giving me the chance to outperform him at fathering. They were allowing me to be a real brother for the first time. They were warming a place inside me that had been cold and dark for a very long time.

We were family now.

The sad thing was that as a man in my mid-twenties, I still didn't really know how to be a real member of a family. I suppose I *wanted* to be a real brother to James and Michael and David—just as I'd wanted to be one to Luke—but my heart had been skating in its same icy ruts for too long.

The way these feelings percolated up to my consciousness was as a vague worry that my relationship with the boys and my passion for Africa were on a collision course. One thing or the other was about to happen: Either my responsibilities to the boys were going to keep me from spending as much time in Africa as I wanted to, or my work in Africa was going to remove me from the lives of my precious little brothers. Either outcome was too horrible to contemplate, so I did what I did best: I avoided the issue. I kept myself in a hamster-wheel maelstrom of work and school and brief, frenzied bursts of play with the boys, and in so doing, avoided thinking about the unthinkable.

7. "A Gun Was Easier to Get Than Books Around There"

MICHAEL MATTOCKS

One day Alvin, Mickey, Little Charles, and me went to Mr. Nat-ly's, a store in the neighborhood, to get some candy. Who walks in but another friend of ours, Mumar. Mumar was all excited and wanted us to come out on the sidewalk to see; he had him a four-five up under his shirt and wanted to show us all. Man, guns was easier to get than books around there. That's cool, we said, and Alvin, Mickey, and I went back in the store to get our candy. Suddenly: BANG! The three of us go running outside, looking this way and that, and don't see nothing. But when we turned around, Little Charles was right there at our feet, fallen against the wall with a big hole in his face. Blood was coming out of him like water out of a water fountain—a big spurt in front and another bigger one out the back of his head. Mumar was just standing there, frozen, tears all over his face. "I can't believe what I just did," he said. "I can't believe what I just did." It was a cold accident, but that didn't keep them from giving Mumar fifteen years. Lost his friend and fifteen years of his life in one second.

I was all fucked up from that for a long time. I loved Little Charles like a brother. This is what started me drinking and smoking weed, and after that the violence didn't bother me one bit anymore.

After Little Charles died, I had nightmares for over a year. I used to drink myself to sleep, hoping I wouldn't be woken up by them bad dreams. I was trying to ease the pain of losing my best friend. That pain was vicious.

Not long after Little Charles got shot, I heard about this dude named Cool. Word was, he was the baddest motherfucker in the neighborhood, and right away I wanted to meet him. Thirteen years old and dealing crack, but already I was bored. A buddy of mine brought me to meet him one day.

Cool turned out to be a grownup, like twenty-two or twenty-three. He was short and stocky, with a light-colored complexion like mine. What made that motherfucker look so evil, though, was his eyes. They were kind of yellow, like cat eyes. He'd look at you straight on, man, and you'd go cold as ice. First time I walked up on him he was like, "What are you doing here? This ain't your part of town," and I was like, "I came down to see what's up with you. I'm tired of that bullshit up there."

"Shorty," he said, "you don't want to hang with me."

"Yes I do."

He looked at me with those evil yellow eyes and then smiled. From under his jacket he took a big-ass gun—a Ruger nine-millimeter—and handed it to me. It was heavy, and warm from being up against his belly. "Let's see what you can do with that."

My buddy took off. He didn't want any part of that shit. But I was going to be a little man and show what I could do. Cool and I took a walk up O Street until we saw shuffling toward us, on the other side of the street, a classic raggedy-assed crackhead.

You can always tell a crackhead; their mouths twitch. This one's mouth was twitching like a motherfucker, and he had the face of a man looking to score. That meant he had a little money in his pocket. I crossed over and walked right up on him. He didn't even notice me coming up on him because all he saw was a little kid. But he sure as shit saw that gun I put up in his face. He reared back with his eyes real big. "Give it up," I said, and he did—two crumpled twenties. My heart felt like a basketball in my chest; I could hardly breathe. Armed robbery!

Cool was watching me from across the street, and I could hear him laughing. As I got back to him across the street, he took the gun from me and put his arm around my shoulders. "You're all right," he said. "Walk with me." We went back to his place, where he gave me a leather jacket, a sharp little hat, and my first gun. I turned it over and over in my hands; I couldn't believe it. My own gun. It wasn't much of one: a .32 revolver with a long barrel—not the kind of gun any real gangster would carry. It was too weak, and it was too awkward to fit easily in your pants or pocket. But it was a real gun, and it was mine.

I said to Cool, "I want you to walk up the street with me, and show the guys who I'm hanging with now." I wanted to be the macho man. He said all right. I put that .32 in my pocket, and we walked up there to where my friends was hanging out—Fred, Gangsta, Bo, Alvin, Mickey, and Big Boo. Big Boo was something, man; he used to panhandle in Georgetown and make like $600 in a day. When they saw me hanging with Cool, they was like, whoa. I was somebody now.

Cool wasn't much of a drug dealer. He sold a little bit, but that wasn't his thing. Cool was a robber. And the people he liked to rob were drug dealers because they had money and it wasn't like they was going to call the police. I was riding around with him one day, and he saw some guys walking with nice jackets. He hit the brakes, jumped out, and not only took those dudes' jackets but pistol-whipped the shit out them, just for the fun of it.

What I loved about Cool was, he was *violent,* and that gave him respect and power in that neighborhood. In the Sursum Corda projects, people would just give him money so he wouldn't rob them. Just by hanging around him, people would treat me with respect, and some people even feared me. His girlfriend used to tell me to stop hanging with him, that I was too young. But I wanted the respect that hanging around him brought me.

Cool was one go-hard motherfucker. So we're sitting in the car outside the McDonald's one time, and Cool has his oowop on his lap. An oowop is an Uzi. I see his eyes suddenly go all cold, and through the windshield there's two guys pulling up in a big dark car to the drive-up. "I know those motherfucking cops," Cool says, and before I can do anything, he gets out of the car and he's on his feet with that oowop in his hands and just blazing away at those poor motherfuckers. Man, they drove off so fast, bouncing off the curbs and shit. They wasn't no cops; they were just two guys trying to get something to eat! Man, there's bullet shells everywhere, and people screaming and crying, and Cool, he gets back in the car and picks up his burger, takes a bite, and we drive off and he's chewing like it's nothing. I loved that shit! He was doing the real thing.

Things back home was kind of falling apart. Don hadn't been doing too good; the drinking was getting the best of him, and he was fighting a lot with my mom. They'd really go at it—screaming and throwing shit. She'd beat up on him with her fists—really whoop his ass—but the thing about Don was, even drunk there was still a nice man in there because he never once hit my mom. And he was still nice to me.

One problem with being only thirteen was that the guy in the neighborhood who had good weed wouldn't sell to me. I had no trouble buying crack, because the guy selling it to me knew I wasn't using it myself. But the weed seller, well, he didn't think kids as young as me should smoke. So I'd say, Don, here's $10. Go get me some of that good weed, and he'd do it, and he'd buy himself a little wine while he was out.

Then his mouth took to twitching, and I knew then we was going to lose him for sure because once they start smoking crack, that's all they have room for in their lives.

One day, my cousin Glen whipped Don's ass. I don't know what set Glen off; he was usually a cool dude. He knew how to draw real nice. But something Don said or did must have pissed him off, because he gave Don a thorough ass-whipping. Not long after that, Don was gone. It took me and James and Sabrina a while to catch on; he wasn't there when we got up to go to school, and wasn't there when we came home, and wasn't there the next day. Gradually we figured out we wasn't going to be seeing Don no more. It was a big deal; we all liked Don. He'd been around a long time.

Uncle Artie was still around though. Still a skinny little motherfucker, and pretty much just hanging around the house all day, drinking. Only now he was doing crack too. And I was the one selling it to him. So it was more than just, "Gimme that eeeyyeee. . . ." Now it was, "Gimme that rock." When my aunts Stella and Glynda got wind of that, they about shouted the roof down, said I was making Uncle Artie sick. So I went to Artie and told him I couldn't get him his crack no more. And you know what he said to me? He said, "I'm going to get it from you or get it from somebody else." Well shit, I kept selling to him. He was going to smoke it anyway, and I might as well be the one who got that money.

And then everybody in the family figured out I was the guy to go to, and pretty soon I was selling to Aunt Evelyn, Aunt Frances, Uncle Mark—anybody who had the money. Then my cousin Glen's baby-mama left him, and he started smoking crack too—crack he bought from me. Thirteen years old, and I was the family drug dealer. I got so out of hand with my mom, she couldn't handle me at all.

Then she got a new boyfriend named Kenny, and things settled down again. Kenny was a cool dude. Older than my mom; he must have been in his fifties. Thick in the body and light-skinned like me. He was bowlegged and missing three fingers off his right hand. But his brother was a master electrician, and Kenny sometimes did a little work for him. Mostly he was a street guy—a drug addict, but a real nice guy. He took care of us real good. Thing is, even with Kenny around my mother wasn't about to control me.

I only went to seventh grade for a week. I started out okay, but after a week I told the teacher, "I'm sick; I want to go home." She sent me down to the principal, and he told me, "You need to go back to your class." I don't know why, but I went off. I guess I was all wired up from dealing on the streets. I jumped up and got right in that man's face and shouted, "I am going to kick your motherfucking ass! I'm going to shoot you!" I was becoming a tough little motherfucker from hanging with Cool. Man, they put me out so fast. . . . I had to spend the rest of the school year on the street.

The one guy who wasn't a drug dealer or doing drugs who cared about me was J.P., but I didn't see him for a long time during all this because he was going back and forth to Africa. Then one day he showed up, and we went fishing with James and David like we'd always done. There I am, standing on the dock back there behind the Watergate Hotel with my little rod in my hands, just like I'm eight years old again, but I'm thinking about my crackheads, and who else is selling their shit on my block—thinking like the little drug dealer I was. Every now and then I'd glance over at J.P., and he'd either be fishing like he was ready to stare a hole in the water, or he'd be sitting scrunched up on the dock with some big book or file open on his lap. I kept waiting for him to ask me what I was up to. I didn't know if he knew about all the shit I was into, and I didn't know how he'd be about it. I was nervous; what if he decided a drug dealer wasn't worth hanging with no more? The one thing I wouldn't have been able to take was J.P. judging me, J.P. being disappointed with me, J.P. rejecting me.

Turns out, J.P. rarely said a word about it. Maybe he didn't know. It was weird, though, that he didn't jump all over this since he was always so full of questions. My mom was telling him that I was dealing, carrying a gun, and not going to school. But right from the beginning, I would pretend that everything was normal, and I convinced J.P. that none of that stuff was true. I convinced him that my mom got it all wrong about what I was doing. I'll bet he was really confused, cause he saw me smiling and acting like a kid with him, just like always. J.P. probably didn't want to believe the stories he was hearing from my mom, so he mostly left the whole thing alone. He just kept everything on the level of the light and the fun. We didn't get serious for more than a minute.

I didn't know if I was relieved or disappointed.

My new mentor now was Cool, and that shit was confusing as hell. One time we're pulling up to his house and this half-naked lady comes running out screaming. "I know that ain't my mom," Cool says, but it is, and she's all fucked up and screaming that some dude in the house had just raped her. Cool gets out of the car and shoots that motherfucker in the head twice as he tries to run out of the house: *Pa! Pa!* Like it's nothing.

That scared me, seeing him do that so cold, but it didn't stop me hanging with him. Because at the same time, he'd take me with him to do fun stuff, just like J.P. We'd go skating—roller skating in the summer, ice skating in the winter. Whooping around all wobble-legged like a couple of little kids. We'd go bowling, and to the arcades. You don't think about it until you're in the life, but drug dealers take time off to have fun just like everybody else. And I think in his own way, Cool loved me.

Much as I loved hanging with Cool, I still had a good side in me, the side that wanted out of all that shit even if I really didn't know it at the time. I remember one day I woke up and thought about it, and said to myself, "I got to stop this shit before somebody kills me." I went to Cool, and he said, "What the fuck you mean you don't want to do bad things no more?" He pulled this gun out and put it up against my head and said, "The only way you're going to get out of this is I'm going to kill your ass. You know too much about it." He scared me right down to my shoes. I really thought he was going to kill me.

JOHN PRENDERGAST

If you had asked me, when Michael was ten years old, if there was a one-in-a-million chance that he'd become a crack dealer, I'd have said, what, are *you* on crack? No way. Not Michael Mattocks. His attitude was so positive. You only had to look at his face to see how sweet and innocent he was. I'd have said Michael would be the last kid from D.C. who'd go down that road. All he ever talked about wanting to do was take care of his mother and his siblings. "J.P.," he'd say every time I saw him. "I can't wait to buy my mother a house. She's had a hard life. She needs my help. I swear to God, J.P., as soon as I can get a job I'm going to move them out of this place and take care of them." What I clearly wouldn't acknowledge was in that environment, with the crummy schools they were stuck in, the fastest way to take care of his family's needs—though risky—was to deal crack.

I'd thought that my teaching Michael to read would give him a head start on school. I'd thought that my example—of a hard-working, scholarly guy who also had a lot of fun—would make him eager for classroom learning. It was part of the illusion that he was really my brother, a *self-delusion* that certainly had no room for any reality that included Michael as a gun-wielding drug dealer. Not after all that I had invested in him, and the superhero story in my subconscious of how I was rescuing him and his siblings from a life of limited opportunities. Without visual evidence, how would I have allowed myself to think anything else but what Michael was reassuring me, that he would never do such things? And while we're at it, how could a brother of mine be anything but a stellar student? Look at Luke!

Luke, though, wasn't being raised every day next to the most infamous housing project in D.C., wasn't living on North Capitol Street with Uncle Artie in that house, wasn't going to schools that looked more like dreary unkempt prisons than educational institutions. It's a measure of how wildly I was overestimating my own influence, and my own importance, that I thought the relatively small number of hours I spent with Michael would counterbalance the chaotic, underfed, survival-of-the-fittest milieu that was his day-to-day reality, replete with poor schools, few jobs, major crime, no investment, and a criminal justice system that focused far more on punishing criminal activities than preventing them.

At the time I certainly understood the "school-to-prison pipeline," but for some reason, in my mind it didn't apply to Michael. Our country seemed comfortable with the idea of suspending from school an at-risk kid with documented family turmoil for a year at the central point of his adolescent development, even though all the evidence I had read showed that an overreliance on suspensions dramatically increased the odds that a kid would fail academically and eventually drop out, with all that entails. I didn't overtly acknowledge it at the time, but drug dealers wouldn't let go of Michael as quickly and easily as the school system did. The dealers clearly saw his motivation and potential, and they were more willing to invest in him than the school system, which just saw another troubled kid. But that's not to say I shouldn't have been there for Michael too. I guess I just had more faith in the institutions around him than I should have.

As for my own situation, the condemned apartment building I was squatting in was crumbling around me, but I didn't want to pay rent. I was earning too little at my job at Bread for the World, and I wanted to save every penny because I had a

vague idea of starting an orphanage somewhere in Africa. But the fact was I needed to make more money. At the time I heard of a city agency that ran group homes for the developmentally disabled, and the agency offered free housing to anybody willing to look after the clients. As a second job, it would be yet another time sink, another emotional commitment, another universe of needy people intertwined with my life. But no burden seemed too heavy, so I signed up.

I ended up moving into a big house with seven men, between forty and sixty years old, each of whom had developmental challenges that had left him at the approximate mental level of a ten-year-old. They could function well enough—dress, do dishwashing and other service jobs—but they needed supervision. Boy, did they need supervision. John and Eddie were twin brothers; Fred, Charles, Johnnie, Mac, and Brew—it was like being a counselor at a summer camp of gray-haired teenage jokesters. I called them the Dream Team, and in my usual

The Dream Team with my aunt and me, from left to right: Freddie, Aunt Joanne, Brew, J.P., John, Ed, and Charles

way I made them the responsibility of everybody around me. When I had to go to Philadelphia, I brought them with me in an agency-supplied van, and my parents entertained and cooked for them. Of course, everybody had a ball. Especially my dad, who—even though I still wasn't communicating much with him—had a whole new audience.

When my cousin got married in Valley Forge, Pennsylvania, and I had nobody to cover for me at the group home, I loaded the whole Dream Team into the agency van with me and brought them along to the wedding, where they sat in the back grunting, coughing, wisecracking, and hissing like a class of unruly boys on the first day of school. There was some disaster at the hotel, I remember—maybe one of them left a bathtub running, or some such, and two rooms were flooded. Of course, I had Michael, James, and their little brother David there too, and they ran wild. I remember there came this moment of peace in the middle of that weekend when neither the kids nor the Dream Team were around and I had a chance to breathe a little. Then I discovered why. The entire Dream Team was bellied up to the hotel bar with Uncle Bud and Aunt Jo, everybody getting roaring drunk while Michael, James, and David were getting into trouble on the other side of the hotel. I've blocked out my memory of the weekend after that.

My visits to Michael and James were changing. Denise occasionally pulled me aside when I showed up, to give me a long earful about all the terrible things Michael was up to. Running with bad kids. Smoking cigarettes. Smoking weed. Playing around with guns. Dealing drugs.

Guns? Dealing drugs? Michael? No way.

Each time Michael's mother would lay out the litany of sins, would I follow up with the relevant authorities? Did I grab Michael and demand some answers? Did I kick his ass around the block for even *thinking* about dealing drugs, or pat him down for a gun? I didn't. I told myself each time that it was a one-off, that Michael had merely been in the wrong place at the wrong time. Sure, he was a little wild in class, and he might have experimented with cigarettes or a little weed—he was a thirteen-year-old boy! And maybe he wasn't the most studious kid. But there was no way Michael Mattocks was dealing drugs or carrying a gun. To me, that incredible light still beamed out of that round face of his. He still had that fibrous core of goodness to him that wanted to look out for his mom and his siblings. I saw what I wanted to see, and moved along.

I couldn't have admitted this to myself at the time, but more than just faith in Michael was operating, and more than simple denial. I was reaching my personal boundary with Michael. My willingness to truly involve myself with him—to accept the kind of responsibility that our years together would have dictated—was clearly lacking. To engage thoroughly with what was going on would have demanded a tremendous investment of time and energy, and my mind wasn't there. It was in Africa. That's where I wanted to be—physically, intellectually, and emotionally. I couldn't have articulated it then—I couldn't even allow myself to be aware of it—but I was making a choice, and Michael was on the losing end.

It's not that I was a complete machine. I was aware of the big emotional holes in my heart even as I stepped around them. Every now and then, though, I was able to tune into my own feelings and express them right. One afternoon I visited my brother, Luke, and his fiancée, Kim, at their home in South Philadelphia. Luke and I were cordial, but neither of us was the first person the other would call to share thoughts. Even over the years, we hadn't become superclose. Sitting in Luke's house, though, I was overwhelmed with admiration for him. He'd chosen a hard and selfless path; he was still a teacher in an under-resourced Philadelphia public high school. And he'd done what I hadn't been able to do—make a deep, permanent, emotional commitment to a wonderful woman.

Before I could think too long, I heard myself telling Luke how much I admired him and cherished him as a brother. What he did on a daily basis at that school deserved real recognition. I told him I hoped we could spend more time together going forward.

When dinner was over, I was walking down Broad Street when I heard my name being shouted. It was Luke, running after me. He ran up, out of breath, and his eyes were wet and shiny. "I just want to tell you how much being your brother means to me," he said, "and how much I look up to you for who you are." I was shocked. Luke had never shared anything with me before, and most certainly nothing about his feelings for me. I opened my arms and we had a deep embrace, a hug that erased those years of distance between us.

As my high school teacher Mr. Woz once wrote to me, "Epiphanies are life's diamonds amid the shards of glass we search through for solutions to emotional wreckage."

It was around this time that I was going up the escalator at the D.C. Metro and from the corner of my eye spotted a woman walking toward the platform. I was not a man given to falling in love; I'd spent too long as the Lizard, and I expended too much energy on my work and the boys, to hive off a piece of my heart that way. I'd had short-term girlfriends, sure, but none of them ever really laid a glove upon my heart since my high school sweetheart had taken a flamethrower to it. And as the self-protective years went by, I had become much more confident with women, and a bit of a hit-and-run artist.

Something about this woman on the subway platform, though, seemed to yank the heart right out of my chest. I found her waiting for the Red Line in the direction I was going and stood next to her. She had caramel-colored skin and long wavy hair; the smell of her—musky and flowery and intensely female—made my vision blurry. The train was taking an unusually long time to come, and I finally worked up the nerve to say hello. She said hello. We started talking and didn't stop, as the train came and we boarded. We reached my stop but I didn't budge; I kept talking, and so did she. We traveled far past my stop—almost to the end of the line—before she got off. As she did, I put a slip of paper with my phone number on it in her hand.

"What's your name?" I asked as the doors slid closed behind her.

"Jean!"

I waited two agonizing days. The receptionist was alerted to page me if a woman named Jean were to call. Finally, the call came, and in my poverty-stricken state, we arranged to meet at a crummy little pizza shop for our first date. She ended up being two hours late, but something told me to wait for her. It wasn't just her looks, beautiful though she was. Ridiculous as it sounds, I'd felt something sitting next to her on the Metro. There was some kind of subsonic communication, or maybe it was on the level of pheromones. Whatever it was, I'd felt a real bond between us. It turned out we both had very intense family stories; her family was shattered in a thousand different ways, and she was as tortured by it, and as eager to figure it out, as I was tortured and curious about my relationship with my father. It became the basis of our relationship—her supporting me in my painful dance with my family, and my supporting her in hers.

My parents loved Jean, and she became my bridge back to my father. She spent many hours with him—just the two of them. I would pass through a room and find them talking—her forehead surrounded by shiny brown ringlets, sometimes almost touching his, crowned by his gleaming white hair. I never asked Jean or my dad what they talked about, but their conversations were long and deep. My dad would often find his more serious side around Jean, with less of his clowning and Irish bluster. He loved to sit and talk with her, heart to heart, like a priestly confessional. Jean seemed to find the secret passage to my father's heart with no effort at all.

Michael and James loved her too; she was very kind to them. But I could always tell that she was holding something back from the boys, even if they couldn't see it. She'd occasionally come along if I was taking the boys to a festival on the Washington Mall, or to a movie that she wanted to see. Mostly, I'd head off to see the boys, and Jean would go off somewhere to study—she was always taking courses. It wasn't very pointed—at least, not at first—but the message to me was: those are your boys, not mine.

8. "I Was Trying to Do the Thing"

MICHAEL MATTOCKS

I guess I wasn't all the way into the life back then, even with all the crack I was selling. I guess some little part of me wanted to live straight, and that's why I told Cool I didn't want to hang with him no more. Because when they sent me back to seventh grade the next school year, I really tried to do the thing. I went to class, and showed up on time. I did the work and read the books. I remember thinking, "Okay, I can do this." But then one day my name came up on the loudspeaker. "Michael Mattocks, please report to the office," and I thought, *what the fuck?* I go down to the principal's office, and he says, "You're too old for seventh grade." I was like, "What? I ain't but thirteen!" He said, "You look too old; you got a mustache; I don't want you to be bullying the other kids. You ought to be in vocational school." I wasn't bullying nobody, and I told him so. But he didn't let me come back.

I felt so bad. Here I was trying to do the thing, and they put me out just for looking like a tough little motherfucker. My mom marched right up to the school, and the principal told her the same thing. They sent me to some vocational school, but I quit that place after two days. So I was done with school at thirteen. Nobody from the school district called, or came to the house. That was that. I ain't been back since.

That shit crushed me. It broke my spirit. Once I finally had got my head right, I really liked going to school.

At this point my life was so fucked up I couldn't go straight if I tried. And I was broke as shit. I was partying way too much. I was drinking and smoking weed, and all my money was going into that. Little Charles getting killed was still affecting me in ways I couldn't even count.

One day I'm hanging out with my buddy D when this big, dark-skinned fat man walks up. He's got glasses and a big bushy beard; an impressive-looking dude. "Son-son," D says to me—everybody called me Son-Son on account I was the youngest dude out there—"Son-Son," D says, "this is Fats. Fats, Son-Son here can pump." That means I could sell drugs good. This Fats looks me up and down; he was a mountain of a man. "You like the life?" he asks me. He's got this deep, rumbling voice and intelligent, warm eyes, as opposed to, say, Cool. I liked him right off.

"I do," I said.

"I'll tell you what," Fats says. "I'll front you five twenties and see how you work them."

I took those five twenties out on the street, and they were gone before the big hand reached three. When I went back, Fats chuckled in a deep, proud, rumbly way that made me feel like I was his son. He took $50 and gave me the other $50. Then he gave me fifteen twenties, and I sold them right quick too.

"Tell you what," Fats says. "Since you pump this shit good, I'll bring you half a ki tomorrow."

And sure enough, at eight o'clock the next morning, there was Fats a tap-tap-tapping on my door. When he took out that half a ki—a white lump about the size of two softballs—my eyes got big as a motherfucker. This was the big time.

"You're going with me, right Shorty?" Fats said. "We're going to do this thing together."

From then on, I had plenty of crack. Some days you had to be out there for hours because there'd be so many guys out there selling. You'd have to be quick and say, "That's my sale; I got him, I got him." But unlike a lot of guys, I was good at it. Here's why: I was *loyal* to selling drugs, you hear me? The main thing that separates a good dealer from a bad one is: Don't talk smart to your crackheads. Make them be loyal to you. Treat them good. Make them feel like they're somebody. Make them feel like you care. Every Friday, I'd buy gallons of liquor and cartons of cigarettes, and I'd set up a table right there on the street. My crackheads would come by, have a drink and a smoke, and they'd know I was looking out for them. They might say, "I'm hungry," and I'd take out $2 and say, "Get yourself a McDonald's."

Little by little I'd get them to work for me. I might give a crackhead fifty joints, which is like $500. Now there's a fifty-fifty chance he'll smoke them all up. But if he does, all I got to say is, "You ain't getting no more until you pay me back." Half of those motherfuckers had been in the Army and shit, and they had pensions. They had money coming in. I knew I could be patient. This is what separated me from the bad hustlers.

Me, I only shot one guy in my whole life, and that was at my older cousin Glen, Aunt Evelyn's son. He was staying with us, but when he was too drunk, or fucked up on crack, my mom would lock the front door against him. One night he's bang-bang-banging on the door, and I got sick of that shit. I took a bucket of water and leaned out the third-floor window and poured it on his head, and he stopped that banging. I forgot all about him being out there.

Couple hours later I go out, and he's waiting there for me by the stairs. Gets me around the neck from behind, and I can't shake him off; Glen knew how to wrestle. I feel myself starting to fall out. I don't know if he means to kill me or what. So I get that .32 out of my belt and *Pa! Pa!* I shoot him twice in the leg. I ran back inside and hid that gun before the police and ambulance could show up. Glen, he was cool. He didn't tell the cops shit. He came out the hospital and apologized, but that wasn't good enough for me. I told him, "You got to walk around with me a little bit, show the cops there's no hard feelings between us." And he did it. Deep down he's a good dude.

Obviously, after Cool put that gun up on my head and said he'd kill me if I tried to stop dealing drugs and robbing people with him, I went right back to it. Did I really think he'd kill me? I don't know. More likely, I was deep-down glad he'd said that so I could go back to the life, because even though there were times I wanted to get out, the truth was, I needed it.

Here's how you know it wasn't just being afraid of Cool that was keeping me in the life. One day this dude walks by on North Capitol wearing this really slick green jacket with leather sleeves. Without even thinking about it, I pulled that long-barreled .32 out of my belt and put it up in the dude's face. "Give me the jacket, motherfucker," I said, even though I only come up about to his chest. I didn't take his money or anything; I just liked the jacket. A week later I see the same dude on the street, in the same place. He walked right past me, and I'm wearing his motherfucking jacket! It pissed me off; he was showing me disrespect. I put one hand on his chest and held the gun down by my leg. "What the fuck you doing up here?" I asked him. "I robbed you just last week! Don't you know better than to stay out of here?" The motherfucker was all, "Don't kill me, don't kill me!" so I let him go. Bitch went home and called the police.

Well, I see them coming fast around the corner, and I ditched the gun, so at least they didn't get me with that. But they took me downtown and strip-searched me and put me in a cell. I'd never been locked up before, and I was nervous. I didn't call my mom though; I didn't call anybody. After a while, this old white lady gets shown in to see me. Her name was Florence, and she said she was my court-appointed lawyer. She was a real nice lady; she must have been about seventy. She asked me what happened, and I told her some bullshit. I remember this: She looked side to side kind of crafty-like, and she said in this real low voice, "I know you robbed him, but I don't want to see you locked up."

Best she could do for me was a month in juvenile hall. It wasn't too bad. I had to put on a sweat suit, and they gave me a toothbrush, some toothpaste, a sheet, and a blanket. I had my own room; it had one window with a cage on it. There was a big lunchroom where everybody ate together and watched TV, played a little Ping-Pong. I never did see the sun that whole month. They never let us outside or let us exercise. But it wasn't too bad. I wasn't scared or anything.

Now here's the part that really tells you that it wasn't being afraid of Cool that kept me in the life. I called my mom from the pay phone in juvie, and she told me Cool was dead;

somebody had shot him in the stomach. I could have walked away from dealing drugs and robbing people the minute I got out, now that I didn't have Cool threatening me to stay with it. In fact, this guy I never seen before came up to me and said, "I shot your boy, and if you try to retaliate on me, I'm going to kill your ass." So I had a double reason to walk away.

I didn't though. I went right back to the street. It's not like you really think you can die when you're fourteen years old. Plus I had Fats giving me the best crack around—that shit was easy to sell. And as my little stop-in at juvie had taught me, the law couldn't really do shit to me. So why should I quit?

JOHN PRENDERGAST

Jean's effect on the relationship between my father and me was remarkable. Dad loved her, without qualifications, and that seemed to soften him on me. The thaw ran both ways; on our visits to the house in Berwyn, I found I could start glancing at my father. I remember times where I would watch him surreptitiously across the room, studying how he had aged, focusing on his every move and mannerism, hauntingly familiar despite the years of interrupted connection. I yearned to reestablish some kind of connection, to rekindle the magic of our early relationship when he was my childhood hero.

Soon I was able to make occasional eye contact with him, but it was hard as the feelings it evoked were at once overwhelmingly positive and negative. There was no big cinematic moment where we suddenly threw our arms around each other, weeping.

And the changes weren't discussed. But everybody in the house could feel it. My dad and I were exchanging words—however few, however tentative—for the first time in twenty years. I owe that to Jean.

Jean and I did disagree about one big thing: the boys. I would argue to her that the investment I was putting into the boys was going to pay off in the long run—that I was more than a role model. I was a stable and reliable source of love. Because I loved them and they loved me, I argued, the example that I set—hard working, studious, concerned about the world—would rub off on them, turn them into good citizens, and raise them above the difficult circumstances in which they were being raised.

Jean thought I was kidding myself. "The minute you leave those boys, they're right back in that destructive environment," she'd say. "You think you can counteract years of upbringing with a few afternoons fishing?"

The arguments between Jean and me took the form of an intellectual disagreement—at least at first—but there was a genuine emotional heat behind it. I thought perhaps that Jean might have been a bit resentful. I would work at the office so hard, then do my second job with the Dream Team, and then when I had a little time off that I might spend with her, I was often off to see the boys. But instead of understanding the frustrations of a lonely partner, I resented her resentment. Couldn't she see how much the boys needed me? But I wasn't good at all at expressing that or at making Jean feel included. My relationship with the boys was a point of contention between Jean and me that never went away.

I was seeing the boys as often as ever, but I could feel a distance opening between Michael and me. He'd stand on the dock behind the Watergate with his fishing rod, and I'd stand there with mine, and long minutes would go by without either of us talking. I didn't want to do my usual thing of asking him questions because I didn't fully trust where those questions would take us. Michael seemed to be thinking the same thing, that if he started talking about his life, he might start owning up to things he didn't want me to know. The few times I asked about the things his mom had told me, Michael earnestly assured me it was all exaggerated.

I didn't press it because on some level I believed this was the natural order of things. I'd taken on Michael and James when they were little kids. That was the relationship I'd signed on to have. In a funny way, I felt okay withdrawing from Michael because he was a teenager now and I'd never signed on to be a brother to a teenager. I was investing more energy and time into his brother David now, another little kid.

In the same way that my father was great with me and Luke when we were little but couldn't handle our getting older, I simply wasn't willing to deal with Michael and his older kid problems involving life choices and moral dilemmas. I didn't know how to deal with his living a secret and scary life of his own. I loved him no less, but I was so unsettled by his becoming a teenager that I nudged our relationship from the deep, intensely connected one we'd enjoyed for years into a zone of superficiality. All I wanted to do with Michael was just pal around and have a good laugh, as we'd always done. Did we have to talk?

Of course, talking was what Michael needed at that moment, and I wasn't there for him.

Then something unfortunate happened on the home front. I was at my mom's house in Philly and we were waiting for Luke to bring Khayree and Nasir over for the day. Luke had skillfully maintained the relationship with the boys that I had foisted on him when I left for D.C., but that day he had been pressed for time so he had decided not to pick up Khayree. I had a bizarre overreaction to Luke's oversight, feeling that I had somehow once again let one of the brothers down, but my self-loathing expressed itself in the form of fury toward my biological brother. His seeming nonchalance was goading me into a temple-busting rage. After an escalating exchange of accusations, I lunged at him and the last official Prendergast brothers' rumble was on.

When it was all over, there were few things left standing in the living room, including Luke and me. To have blamed Luke for my own shortcomings with Khayree, an extension of my neglect of Michael's real-life challenges, was absurd and unfair. It was typical me: biting off way more than I could chew, getting those around me to pitch in and help, walking away and leaving it to others, and then if it didn't work in my absence, blaming those that only tried to help.

9. "That Shit Is Fun"

MICHAEL MATTOCKS

You wouldn't think so, since I'd lost my buddy Little Charles to a gun accident, but a thing I really liked about the life was the guns. These two Chinese guys used to drive around in a BMW, with their trunk full of them. Nines. Four-fives. I'd thrown away that .32, but shit, $300 or $400 would get you whatever you wanted. I had a nine, and a four-five, and a MAC, which is a compact little submachine gun. Weren't many AKs around in them days; that came later. I used to walk around with my buddy Tony's sawed-off pump shotgun up under my coat. I had the barrel in my pocket and the butt up under by my shoulder. We'd rob crackheads with it. We'd only get like $50 or $60, but it was the fear in their faces when I'd whip that big thing out that I liked. Respect, man. Fear and respect.

There was this summer night I'm standing on North Capitol with seven of my friends. It's about two o'clock in the morning, and you should see how the women dress up there on those hot nights! Anyway, we're out there, drinking our beer and smoking our weed and just chilling, and we see these four dudes coming up in hooded sweatshirts and skullcaps. We know they're strapped; wearing hoodies and it's 90 degrees? But there's too many of us, so they just go by; them eyefucking us and we eyefucking them. So they go past, and we get our guns and run around the corner real quick, so that when they get in their car, we're there. Two of them see us and jump out, pulling their guns out, and it's like *Pa! Pa! Pa! Pa!*—must have been about fifty shots. We shot at them, and they shot at us. Bullets going everywhere, and nobody got hit. They drove off, and we ran around to hide our guns and get back on the stoop in front, laughing like a motherfucker. When you're fourteen years old, that shit is *fun!*

We did a lot of shooting, but hardly anybody ever got hit. It's not like we ever took our guns to the range and practiced with them. What you'd do, if someone got in your face the wrong way—disrespected you, eyefucked you in a way you didn't like—you might peel off a few in his direction. If you hit him, good. But it didn't really matter most of the time because even if you didn't put one in him, you'd said something. You'd said you had the power. You'd made yourself *heard*. There was a time I was shooting my gun at least once a week. Sometimes I'd just shoot it for fun. I liked doing that when I was sitting on the toilet; I'd open the window and shoot out, just to hear it go bang.

Aside from Cool, Little Charles' big brother, Stick, was one of the few people I knew who'd actually killed somebody on purpose with a gun. He was a couple years older than me, maybe seventeen. He was tall and slim and brown-skinned, and had this big round face. I think losing his little brother made him crazy mean, because he never was the same after that. One night he saw this homeless dude bedding down in his mother's backyard, and he killed him with a pump gun. Two days later he was back out on the street. He'd paid his bond and that was that. He was a juvenile, and the guy he killed was some homeless dude; nobody gave a shit.

All of us carried guns. We'd trade them around like baseball cards. Back then there was this guy going around killing people with a shotgun—the "Shotgun Stalker" is what they called him in the paper. That dude was scary because he had no reason for what he was doing. He'd pull up to someone on the street and BAM! Just random. We used to stand around on the corner wishing he'd come by and try to get one of us. Man, we'd have lit that motherfucker *up!*

One day, I bought a gun from a drug addict in my neighborhood for $40. It was a Colt .38 snub-nose; a nice little gun. I thought I'd taken all the shells out of it and was sitting on my bed with James click-click-clicking it when suddenly the bitch went off. Bullet went right past James' head and up into the wall. Man, my mom came running in, all drunk, like, "What the fuck is going on?" She didn't take the gun from me though. Kenny, he just laughed. He was a cool dude.

I wish Mom had taken that gun away because not long after that I was standing in front of my house in the early morning when I see a police officer over here walking my way, and three more over there looking at me, and I'm thinking, *uh oh.* Then a police car pulls up right in front of me, and a whole mess of them jump out, and I'm thinking, What the hell do I do now? I got that .38 in my jacket pocket. I turn to go inside, but the door is locked. My mom always put me out in the morning and wouldn't let me back inside until three, even though she knew I wasn't going to school. I guess she thought if I was out of the house during school hours, she could pretend like I was going to school. All I know is, that door was locked, and by the time I turned around, all those police were right on top of me. "Why aren't you in school?" they asked me.

"I'm sick," I said.

"Bullshit," one of them said. "Take your hands out of your pockets."

I took the left one out but kept the right in the pocket on top of the gun.

"Other one," the cop said. He had his hand on his gun now, and I knew that if I came out with that gun in my hand, they'd shoot me dead right there.

"It's broke," I said.

"I'm going to pull it out," he said.

"Well, then that's what you're going to have to do."

He pulled my arm and my hand came out with the gun in it. I think they were all so surprised they froze for a split second, and in that split second I broke free and ran. They didn't catch me for another month; I made sure to come and go only at night. They got me finally, and then I found out why they were so interested in that gun. It was a police detective's gun. It had been taken from him in a bank robbery. They took me downtown in front of a judge, and they tried to get me to tell them who'd sold me the gun. I told them, "A drug addict."

"Which one?"

"I don't know. A drug addict."

We went round and round like that for hours. I wasn't going to rat out one of my own crackheads; that wouldn't have been right. The police tried getting tough, telling me I was going to grownup prison, but I knew that was bullshit; I wasn't but fifteen years old by then. There really wasn't nothing they could do to me, and they knew it. So they tried making nice. They had a lady detective there named Davis, and she said she'd get me into a GED program at University of the District of Columbia.

I went to the program, even though I never did tell them where I got the .38. But then I dropped out. I was making too much money dealing drugs to bother with getting a GED. What was I going to do with that? Get a $6-an-hour job?

It felt weird when J.P. came by to pick me, James, and David up. David had been coming along for a couple years now. He was ten now, four years younger than James. From the time David started coming with us, J.P. was covering him with questions—Who's your favorite player? Who's the cutest girl in the second grade? What did you eat for dinner last night?— like he used to do with me. To me, though, he'd just say, "Hey, buddy." I waited for his questions. I had answers all ready if he'd have asked if I was dealing, or carrying a gun. But he rarely asked anything.

J.P. had had a lot of girlfriends over the years who he'd some- times bring along on our outings, but I could tell this new girl, Jean, was something special to him. He was quieter around her. He acted less goofy. She was real sweet to me and my brothers, and when it was all of us together, we did different kinds of things—like outdoor art shows down on the Mall in front of the Capitol building and shit like that. She didn't come with us too much though.

It was a mixed-up time for me. Playing around with James and David, or fishing with our little rods, was starting to feel like little-boy shit. I was a man now. So there came a day when J.P. pulled up in that big ugly car of his, and while David and James ran down the front steps as happy as they could be, I just stood up there with my arms folded. Naw, I said. Not today. I'm not going today.

"You sure?" J.P. said. He was standing by his open car door, leaning on the roof.

"Yeah, I'm sure," I said. I think I expected J.P. to beg me to come along. I think, deep down, I hoped he was worried about all the shit I was doing and would drag me away from it. I wanted him to love me that much.

"Okay, buddy," he said, and he gave me a little salute. Then he climbed in the car and drove off with James and David.

I felt good and bad at the same time watching him drive off. Good, because I was a man now, through with that little-boy shit, independent. But sad that something real good was leaving my life. I'd been hanging with J.P. for nearly nine years. Those outings of ours had been a big part of my life, something that made me different from all the other knuckleheads up and down the street. I had Mr. and Mrs. P in my life, Luke, Uncle Bud, and Aunt Jo. There'd been a whole lineup of J.P.'s friends—from Geoff and John up to Jean. As I stood watching that car of his disappear around the corner of O Street, I didn't know if all that was leaving my life for good. Then David and James would come back from their adventures with J.P. that I wasn't going on anymore, saying, "We did this! We did that!" and I'd get all sad. I wanted to be with J.P. and I didn't, and it had me all confused.

One night, it all got on top of my ass. Suddenly, I was tired—but I mean, like, deep tired. Tired of the stress on the street. Tired of the drugs. That image of my buddy Little Charles with that big hole in his face, was popping up in front of my face every day. All the fun had gone out of it and left behind nothing but the terror and the meanness and the despair of those streets and those crackheads. I was sitting on my bed with the door closed and the lights out, drinking one Saint I's after another and smoking a ton of weed. In my lap was a gun I'd borrowed from a friend—a nickel-plated .38 snub-nose, fully loaded with hollow-point bullets. When I was so drunk and stoned that I figured I'd feel no pain, I brought that gun up to my head and pulled the trigger. It went click, and I passed out.

Next morning, I took that gun out to the alley behind our house, pointed it into a pile of trash, and pulled the trigger. It fired. I pulled again and it fired again. I shot off all six; the gun worked perfectly. I threw it in the Dumpster and walked away, shivering—like something bigger than me knew I wasn't supposed to die that way at fifteen.

I never told J.P. about that. Never told anybody, in fact, until now.

JOHN PRENDERGAST

After years of running in every direction and grazing aimlessly, I now knew in what direction I wanted to march. My goal—and it hasn't changed to this day—was to help guide U.S. policy toward relieving some of the worst suffering in Africa, particularly resulting from the wars there. So I knew I was going to have to devote myself now to two parallel pursuits: returning to African war zones as often as possible and learning as much as I could back home about U.S. foreign policy as it related to peacemaking and the protection of human rights. Where are the real levers of power in Washington, I wanted to know, and how does one learn to pull them?

Washington was, and is, full of nongovernment organizations, or NGOs as they're called, focusing on hunger, AIDS, children, human rights, trade, the environment, peace, and on and on. All these issues touch Africa. And as I went around visiting, I found that a lot of them were glad to find a guy willing to travel to the most dangerous corners of the continent for them. All those years I spent cramming books into my head and writing complicated graduate-level papers at the last minute had prepared me well for the relatively easy task of writing up reports for an NGO, and it turned out that my ability to produce clear writing on a deadline was every bit as valuable to these organizations as my willingness to take dangerous and uncomfortable trips. Word spread among them that I could get the job done, and suddenly I had all the work I wanted in all of Africa's most violent war zones. I would go in, listen to the people most affected by the conflict, and conspire with them on constructive solutions. Then I would come back to the United States and try to package what I had learned into messages that might move policy-makers to do something in response.

If I wasn't focused on how violent Michael's life had become, perhaps it was partly because violence was touching my own life in terrifying ways. On one trip to southern Sudan, I came as close to thinking the end was as near as it could possibly be. I'd flown from northern Kenya into rebel-held southern Sudan aboard a small plane, as I often did. I was trying to be discreet, though, because I'd recently coauthored a book for Human Rights Watch that assessed the human rights situation in Sudan, and it contained a tough critique of the rebels' human rights record. (The Khartoum government of Omer al-Bashir was immeasurably worse, and we had covered that comprehensively, but criticizing only the government in the book would have been irresponsible and incomplete.) I doctored an expired entry visa for rebel territory, and I hoped to slip in unnoticed. But small planes were rare at the flyblown strips where I used to land, and a small crowd of rebel soldiers was there when I stepped out. Two of them grabbed my arms, and, speaking to each other in Dinka, they frog-marched me to a nearby town and threw me in a small shipping container that doubled as a jail. Nobody explained anything. A can of filthy water was put inside with me, which, since it was like an oven in there, I drank, with predictably disastrous results. The rebel soldiers told me in broken English, "Nobody knows you're here, so nobody will know if you die here." I spent three days in that makeshift jail—roasting, sick, deprived of food, and certain I was about to be executed. Finally, the late rebel leader John Garang ordered my release.

This wasn't the only brush I had with my mortality. Over the years, I was shot at in Somalia, had a gun stuck in my mouth on the Rwanda/Congo border, detained and roughed up by government security agents in Zimbabwe, missed by a rocket in a plane over Sudan, had a car in front of me blow up running over a land mine in Angola, was in a building in Somalia that was hit by a mortar and partially collapsed, and was taken captive by a militia in Congo in the middle of the night when no one knew where I was.

On what I think one could call a lighter note, once one of my frequent indiscretions got the better of me, as I spent the night in a tent in a remote corner of a war zone with a striking aid worker. It rained all night, and she and I woke up in the morning in the middle of a swamp with a crocodile staring through the screen into the tent. Eventually the water receded and another proverbial bullet was dodged.

This kind of stuff came with the territory, and I was prepared for anything. Ironically, Michael didn't know I was facing such violence (and crocodiles) in my travels, and I didn't want to deal with the fact that he had entered a very violent world of his own. The parallels were stark, had we only realized and catalogued them: violence, women, altercations, adrenaline addiction, defiance in the face of danger, trying to take care of people, wanting admiration, and on and on. Both of us had lost friends on our respective battlefields, whether on contested drug corners in D.C. or war zones in Africa. We would have had a lot to talk about, if we'd have just sat on the steps one day and compared notes about how we both were forced to normalize the insanity that surrounded us.

One of the shared emotional experiences that we never spoke of all those years but that tied Michael and me together was the childhood trauma we both experienced. Both of us at an early age were deprived somehow of our fathers' protection. We both felt at a young age, because of this, an acute lack of power to change the unfairness surrounding us. We attempted to fill the holes in our hearts in very opposite ways: I reacted proactively by fighting to bring voice to others; Michael reacted defensively by becoming someone feared and respected so that he would never be disempowered by anyone again.

In northern Uganda I once befriended a former child soldier who had recently escaped from captivity and who had endured some of the worst horrors I had ever heard from my years in the war zones. Seeing his hard eyes, cool demeanor, dangling cigarette, and ever-present vaguely concealed weapon, I couldn't help but think how similar these child soldiers in Africa were to the child soldiers in the streets of D.C., making money for older people who are willing to use them as pawns, in a world that isn't even trying to address the causes of this outrage, and who are perfectly willing to punish the children for their crimes.

Anyway, as soon as I'd get off a plane from Africa back in the United States, I'd stay awake for a night or two writing up the report for whichever NGO had financed the trip, and then I'd recycle what I'd learned for articles and op-ed pieces that I tried to place anywhere. I always tried for the big-name papers, but I would settle for just about any place in print. When the *Washington Post* finally accepted a full 800-word opinion piece from me, I was beside myself with glee because it would appear right in the center of American power.

Back in the pre-Internet days, once you learned your piece was accepted by the *Washington Post*, you'd have no idea when it would run. So every night at 2 A.M., I'd walk down to the 7-Eleven to wait for the new day's paper to arrive. The late-night clerk at the 7-Eleven was Ethiopian, and when the bundles came flying off the truck, he and I would each grab a copy and turn the pages furiously to get to the op-ed page. Weeks went by like this, until one morning the article suddenly appeared. The 7-Eleven clerk and I rejoiced, and my coauthor Almami Cyllah from Amnesty International and I were asked to do a number of press interviews that day, magnifying our message.

I imagined our words ringing through the halls of power, awakening the conscience of the nation, and changing the course of history.

How blissfully naïve I was.

It would take a lot more than one op-ed to move people, and I learned quickly that stopping genocide and promoting peace wasn't like fixing a streetlight. It would take a patient, long-term commitment to real change.

Regardless, every byline, no matter the paper, was a victory—not for me, but, in my mind, for Africa. If each article made one American care about the destructive wars and famines far across the ocean, I'd have been happy. (To my mother, of course, the bylines were gold stars on little J.P.'s homework papers. She framed the first one from her local paper, the *Philadelphia In-*

quirer.) Between my trips to Africa, and my halting attempts to get the American power structure to listen, I was little by little figuring out issues of war and peace in Africa and what the U.S. government could do to help. A personal ambition began forming in my mind: Maybe by the time I'm fifty, if I had learned enough, I could be a desk officer for some war-torn African country at the State Department.

Whenever I was home, no matter how briefly, I'd get up to North Capitol Street to see the boys. David continued to come along, and he was just the easiest, sunniest, and most pleasant little guy in the world. He wasn't at all prone to the dark, violent rages that would come upon James at surprising moments. He was more the way Michael had been as a little boy. And for that reason, it was probably easier for me than it should have been to let Michael go. Michael was fifteen years old, old enough to make his own decisions, whereas David was very eager to listen and to do all the things kids love to do.

One day when I drove up, Michael was on the stoop with his arms folded; James and David ran eagerly for the car. Michael nodded but didn't move. Then Denise burst out of the front door and pulled me inside.

"That boy's out of control," she proclaimed. "You got to do something."

I closed my eyes. I just couldn't listen to more horror stories about Michael.

"Dealing them drugs, got a gun up under his shirt. Almost shot his brother by accident here in the house one night."

As Denise went on and on about all the terrible things Michael had done since I'd last been there, I felt a coldness drop
over me like a sodden blanket. This is what my father used to go
through—a long complaint from my mom about all the terrible
things the kids had done the minute he walked through the door
from a business trip. I was starting to understand him. I could
see why he'd fly into a rage. Thing is, it wasn't Michael I felt myself growing angry at; it was Denise. Maybe it was that way for
my father too, but instead of snapping at Mom, he turned it all
on me instead. I pushed down the anger and tried to brush off
everything she was saying.

"Come on, Denise. . . ."

She grabbed my arm. "I got nobody here to help me with
that boy," she said. "He's going to end up dead in the gutter if
you don't do something."

I gave her some vague assurance of my concern and went
back outside to take James and David off to play. But not before
Uncle Artie loomed up from the shadows to touch me for a few
dollars. What a household that was.

Michael was standing on the stoop when I got outside. He
hadn't grown very tall, but he'd filled out the way young men
do. His shoulders were broad now, his arms muscular. He had a
little beard and his hair was in corn rows.

"Hey, buddy," I said. "You're not dealing drugs, are you?"

"No."

"And you're not carrying a gun?"

"No."

"Okay then," I said, and shrugged. Michael and I bumped
fists, I saluted him as I got into the car, and James and David
and I went off to have our fun.

10. Amazing Grace

MICHAEL MATTOCKS

I'd just turned seventeen when I was out in front of the house one day doing my thing. Up rides Little Charles' brother Stick on his bicycle. I asked could I borrow the bike for five minutes so I could ride down to the store for a bag of chips and a soda. I'm gone five minutes, and as I ride back, I see someone lying on the sidewalk. When I get up close, I see it's my mom's boyfriend Kenny, with blood all over his shirt. Stick turns to me, and is like, "Give me my motherfucking bike," and he's gone. Kenny is lying there breathing heavily, and then he gives one big breath and dies while I'm standing right there. I look up and I see my little brothers James and Tyrell looking out the window; they'd seen the whole thing.

Well, the police come, the detectives start talking to James and Tyrell, who are fifteen and eight. I'm responsible for them, because they're my little brothers, and my mother is in no kind of shape.

I look up and down the street, at people watching my little brothers talking to the police, and I know that isn't good. So I get up in the faces of those detectives, and I say, "You need to get away from my motherfucking house." If James and Tyrell were to rat out Stick, or Stick even thinks that, Stick's people are going to come back and kill them. I know that, and those *detectives* know that. But they don't give a fuck. They just want James and Tyrell to tell them who stabbed Kenny. I'm getting hot. I explain, "You're going to get my little brothers killed standing out here on the front stoop talking to them." Finally, they back off, and I'm like, good. Be gone. But then I hear something, and I run around back of the house, and there the detectives are, talking to James and Tyrell at the back door. I flicked off, screaming, "You are putting my family in danger. You are going to get my brothers killed!" It's a wonder they didn't take me downtown. What they did was hustle James and Tyrell out of the house, put them in the patrol car, and take them to the police station. Got the whole story from them when I wasn't around.

People on the street said what happened was Stick was playing with Kenny, picking on him, and Kenny kept telling him to stop. Stick wouldn't stop, so Kenny punched him in the face. They say Stick went into the barbershop there, got a pair of scissors, came out, and stabbed Kenny with them a bunch of times. Then he ran back in the barbershop and washed off the blood before the police could get there and before I could see.

I felt bad about all that. Stick and Kenny were both good dudes and never was beefing with each other before. I guess they were just having a bad day.

Before James saw Kenny get killed, he was still in school, riding bikes and skateboarding around the neighborhood. James, though, was close to Kenny. He saw Kenny take his last breath, and that really fucked him up. He stopped riding bikes and doing kid stuff. Seeing Kenny get killed was a major turning point for James. That's when I started bringing James out hustling with me. I wanted him close by me, to protect him. James was fifteen, and on those streets, fifteen is a man. It wasn't like he was begging me to go out in the streets with me. But when I gave James a .22 pistol, he was so excited to have his own gun the clip kept falling out of it. When I went out to sell my crack, I brought James with me. I kept him right there by my side all the time. Brought him into the life to keep him safe, and look what happened.

John Prendergast

After a few years of somewhat volatile and on-and-off dating, Jean and I finally decided to get engaged. When I was going shopping for an engagement ring, I asked Luke and my old U. Penn buddy Adam, who was a real sharp business whiz, to accompany me in case my feet got too cold. Of course, the Dream Team had to come along too, as I had brought them up to Philly with me that weekend. I'll never forget the rattled jeweler showing us dozens and dozens of stones, as the Dreamers kept arguing, grunting, and hissing over each and every option, all of them taking it as seriously as if they were going to be walking down the aisle instead of me.

Jean and I were married in 1991, so now it wasn't just a girlfriend relationship I was trying to keep alive; it was a marriage. By this time, I was living in two worlds. I would spend about half my time in Africa, working for different human rights and humanitarian organizations, moving through war zones and learning as much as I could. And when I wasn't physically in

Africa, I was mentally in Africa. Jean was studying nutrition at the time, and she had a career to launch; she wanted my involvement and support. But even though my parents had stayed together, I hadn't learned from my dad any secrets of keeping a marriage real and alive over the long term. If he'd had lessons to impart, neither of us was in a space to let that happen, even though we were moving toward reconciliation thanks to Jean.

I was consumed with Africa, and the unspeakable suffering I saw in the war zones I was visiting and working in. Any time I took away from learning more about it, or writing about it, or networking on Capitol Hill and in the halls of power around Washington, felt to me like an affront to the people there—the refugees and mass rape survivors who so earnestly would implore me to go back to Washington and get the American government involved in helping to make peace. One after another, in refugee camps and destroyed villages, the frontline witnesses would describe to me the horrors they had experienced and look at me with hope that their story would be heard somewhere that mattered. How could Jean's need for a functional relationship compare with that?

As for the boys, I was now really enjoying my relationship with David. David had become a truly phenomenal athlete. He was only ten or so at this point, but we had a great time playing basketball together. Down on the border of Southeast D.C. and Maryland, off of Pennsylvania Avenue, was an old Lowe's warehouse converted to an indoor complex, a basketball Mecca, with about fifteen courts laid side by side. I had never seen anything like it before. The courts were open twenty-four hours a day, and every time we'd be there in the middle of the night, all the courts would be full. David had amazing strength and grace.

A few years later, we'd be playing, and guys on the other courts would stop to watch him; he was that good. A lot of young men dream of playing professional basketball, as I did. Great as they are on the playground court, most of them don't have anywhere near the skills to play professionally. David had a shot at making it to the NBA if he'd had the slightest bit of ambition or discipline.

Michael had stopped coming on our outings altogether. Denise would torment me, every time I showed up, with tearful pleadings to help Michael. I would leave trying to come up with a plan to help him, but it would peter out, losing in the competition with my Africa work and, frankly, with my own ambivalence about getting more deeply involved in his life.

As for James, what had been a bothersome temper when he was little had become a disturbing darkness. He was a fully grown teenager now, so whatever violent streak he harbored could now do real harm. I didn't fear for my own safety; we were too close for that. But he was difficult to be around. His eyes sometimes took on a hooded coldness, and I worried about being witness to something truly awful.

I'd often think: I should go see the boys. But there'd be so many Africa reports to read and write, and never enough time for Jean, and many times in this period I'd let the moment go by.

A lot of the time I'd be plain beat, and I would simply lie on my bed watching a basketball game. Babies are dying in Africa, Michael is disappearing into the streets, and the self-styled superhero is lying on his bed watching hoops. It's amazing I could concentrate on a basketball game at all.

11. "Old Enough to Be a Drug Dealer, Young Enough to Cry"

MICHAEL MATTOCKS

I was sitting on my bed when James came up the stairs crying. I thought maybe some kid had pushed him down or some shit. He sounded like a little boy.

"Uncle Mark took my shit!" he wailed.

"Say what?"

Uncle Mark was one of my mother's thirteen brothers and sisters, a big tall motherfucker, and just as useless as the rest of them. He didn't work. He just kind of hung around, living off my mom, buying drugs, kind of an all-around fuck-up. James took me downstairs, to where we had a dresser that stood in the front hallway of the house. James used to keep his drugs in that top drawer, and now it was empty.

Damn. Uncle Mark had already ripped me off once—took $1,000 and 150 joints out of my dresser one time. I hadn't had any proof, though, and I'd let him off that time. Shit, he towered over me. If I was to do something to him, it would have to have been with a gun.

James stood looking down at that empty dresser drawer with tears on his face. He wasn't but fifteen years old—old enough to be a drug dealer on North Capitol Street, Washington, D.C., but young enough to cry when somebody stole his shit.

We went out looking for Uncle Mark, and he wasn't hard to find. I backed him into an alley and put my .38 to his head and my nine to his chest. "You give my brother his shit back."

Uncle Mark's eyes got real big, like he didn't know whether to laugh or have a heart attack. "I don't know what you're talking about," he said.

I shot twice in the air, right next to his face, and Uncle Mark began whimpering. James was standing next to me, and he got this funny little smile on his face and a genuinely scary coldness took over his eyes. "Let's kill this nigger," he said in a kind of low growl. I looked at him, like, *what the fuck you talking about? Kill Uncle Mark?*

I looked up at Uncle Mark, who was muttering, "You ain't going to shoot me. You ain't going to shoot me."

I thought: He's right. I'm not going to kill this nigger. Funny thing is, I wasn't even thinking about prison. I was thinking about my mom, and how mad she'd be if I killed her little brother. I told Uncle Mark to beat it, and he scurried off like a rabbit. James was pissed, waving his little .22 around. "We shoulda *killed* him!" he kept saying, and I had to say, "James, James. Cool down, man."

James always had a temper as a kid; I knew that. I guess I thought it's the kind of thing he'd outgrow. But he held onto it and turned it into a scary grownup thing. And if you think about it, North Capitol Street was the worst possible place to have a temper, because that shit can be lethal up there.

One day he and I were walking with Sabrina. We liked having Sabrina around because she carried our guns in her purse;

the cops was less likely to search a girl. Also, if any shit went down, you wanted Sabrina there with you, just like when we were kids. She not only had James' .22 and my .38 in that purse, she had a big shiny .357 Magnum that she just loved. She could handle it too, little as she was. And wasn't shy about whipping it out either.

We're walking along and we pass a dude leaning on some crutches. Just some scruffy guy on the street, a guy we don't know. He whistles at Sabrina. Men often did that; she's real good-looking. Sabrina let it go, but James got that same weird little smile on his face like he did when we were shaking down Uncle Mark.

"Nigger," he said, "that's my motherfucking sister." Next thing I know, James has snatched away the guy's crutches and has him down on the ground, really whipping his ass with one of them. I knew better than to try to pull him off. We leave that guy there bleeding and unconscious, and I'm wondering what the fuck is up with James. We were so close. We'd sleep in the same bed. We'd drink Nyquil and smoke weed every night before going to sleep. But there were times when I still didn't feel like I knew what the fuck he was thinking.

With Don chased off and Kenny dead, it seemed like things was falling apart for us. Stick was facing thirty to life for stabbing Kenny with those scissors. He called me one time from jail during the year that they held him while he was waiting for his trial, and this is what he said to me: "I hope your brothers die."

That was it for me. Once James and Tyrell were identified as witnesses to Kenny's murder, we couldn't stay up on North Capitol no more. Besides, that house of ours was full of rats. It was time to go.

I was almost seventeen by now, a full-grown man. My mom found us a nice house up on Georgia Avenue. The house on North Capitol was rat-infested, and they told her to leave. She got subsidized rent, and I paid all the bills and helped out with my brothers and sisters. It was two-story, brick, in a long row of identical attached houses. It had a porch we could set on and look straight across Georgia Avenue at Walter Reed Army Medical Center. It was nice up there—quieter than North Capitol, and a lot less nasty, being far from Sursum Corda. Turned out, moving into that Georgia Avenue house changed my whole life because something happened that very first day that is still a big part of me today.

We was carrying our stuff inside the house and this dude walks up, introduces himself as Chris, and offers to help us unload the cars. When we were done working, Sabrina went over to his house, and while she was there she met his sister, Nikki. Sabrina liked what she saw; Chris and Nikki lived a normal life, with two parents in the home, and neither Chris nor Nikki had any connection to the life. Nikki had her a newborn baby boy, Rolando. Sabrina sees all this, and she says to Nikki, "I got a brother you might like."

Sure enough Nikki comes around the house one day not long after. I see a nice-looking girl, nicer looking than most of the women I was currying with at the time. And sassy as a motherfucker. I could see that girl had a good head on her. I was interested, sure. But I wasn't ready for this: That very first day I met her, Nikki says to me, "I don't got time to be bullshitting, but I want you to be my boyfriend." I figured she was just talking shit. She'd only just met me, and she probably knew I was a drug dealer right off. So I say, "Sure." I'm joking around. I had so many women then. Turned out, though, she was serious. And I mean, like, *serious.*

Here's how serious: I went to jail right around then, and Nikki stood by me the whole time. What happened was, me and James were still going down to North Capitol every day to sell our drugs because we had all our crackheads down there and we knew those streets. But one day, we're up in the new house on Georgia Avenue smoking PCP and got to fighting with each other. Sabrina, she came in and tried to bust us up, and, being all fucked up on PCP, I pulled my .38 out and cocked it. "Anybody touches me again, I'll kill 'em," I said. (That PCP will fuck you up.) My mother's watching all this, her kids pulling guns on each other, and she freaks out and calls the police. I hear her doing that and run upstairs to hide the gun, but somehow it ended up on my bed all tangled up in the sheets. Well, the police show up, find the gun right off, and take me downtown. I played crazy so they sent me to St. E's—that's St. Elizabeth's, the mental hospital for criminals. I was in there only three weeks, 'cause I was still a juvenile. Being around crazy people was hard. But it was better than D.C. jail, believe me.

Not long after I got out, I was hanging with Nikki on the porch of the Georgia Avenue house. Just chilling there in my shorts, when the federal marshals drive up. "Is Mr. Mattocks home?" they ask. I figure they're there about the gun charge, and I get up to get the paperwork inside the house, show them that that beef is already taken care of. They stop me and say, "This isn't a gun charge; this is murder."

Murder? Me? Turned out they had word of a murder down on North Capitol, and they thought I could tell them about it. But I wasn't having any part of that. So they locked me up in the D.C. jail, and man, that bitch was hard. Dirty. Filthy. Roaches. Horrible food. You got this hard-ass little mattress. You never get outdoors. Guys fighting. James was in there at the same time as me; they were holding him to make him talk about seeing Kenny murdered, even though it happened a few months before, but now Stick's trial was coming up. They left Tyrell alone cause he was too young. A guy came up to me in there and said that three guys had jumped James—jumped him a couple of times—and he'd just laughed at them. That was James. They fucked with him a few times, he gave one of them an ass-whipping, and after that they left him alone.

Nikki visited me every day while I was in the jailhouse, wrote me lots of letters, and accepted all my phone calls. She even sent me a little bit of money. I never had a woman do that for me before, and I didn't hear from anybody else the whole time I'm inside. It was cold when I got out; they'd kept me in there ninety days. Nikki was waiting for me right there and took me home. I'm starting to think this is one nice girl. She wasn't with the bullshit. Finished school. Had her a little job. Did nice things for me—even threw me a party on my birthday. Nobody'd ever done that. I said to her, "Why do you want me? I'm a no-good-ass nigger. I got nothing." And she said, "I'm not tripping off that." And this all before we'd even had sex! I didn't have sex with Nikki for seven months. *Seven months!* I was used to getting females the first night, or the first week. Nikki was a challenge; I liked that.

So I cut back all the other women, and I started hanging full time with Nikki. I'd never had a girl with a baby before. She said to me, "If you accept me, you have to accept my child." And I did. From that day I treated Rolando like my own son. Nikki ended up moving out from her parents' and into her own apartment, and she asked me, do I want to move in with her and little Rolando. I said, "No, I want to stay home with my mom." But I helped her move, and then I never went back home.

Still haven't.

Nikki's dad, Cleo Jackson, was everything the men in my family weren't. He worked hard at one job his whole working life, as a crane operator. He was married to one woman his whole adult life, Miss Sandy. He was very clean-cut, with dark skin and glasses, and a quiet, dignified manner. One night not long after I got out of jail, he sat me down.

"You've got to straighten your life out, son."

"I know, sir."

"I don't want to hear about you being mean to my daughter. You respect that child."

"Yes, sir."

"A woman is a big responsibility for a man. You need to give up these streets and get yourself a real job, that you can do your whole life until you're old."

It went on like that for four hours. I think he drank maybe two Budweisers the whole time. He talked to me about man things, but not like he was talking down to me. He knew what I was doing on the street, but he wasn't judging me. I think, like Nikki, he could see the good in me. And he knew that Nikki loved me and that I was falling in love with Nikki. He had faith in me, faith that because I loved his daughter, I'd leave the life and straighten myself out.

That man showed me a tremendous amount of respect, and I've never forgotten that.

It wasn't like one conversation was going to completely change my life though. When I got out the D.C. jailhouse, I told James, "We're not going back down to North Capitol anymore. We're going to stay up here." I could see there was more money up on Georgia Avenue. Also, there were fewer people selling, which meant less pressure, less jealousy. Plus, the ones selling up on Georgia Avenue were uptown niggers, and we were downtown niggers. We were rough. We had a style—sagged pants and a tough look. Uptown niggers are pretty boys. They knew we were from downtown, what kind of news we was.

My buddy Fats found us this new kind of crack one day, called Fish Scale, and he brought a little bit up there. Right away, people were like, "You got more? You got more?" I called Fats and said, "We need more of this." Now, I didn't like people fronting me shit. If I couldn't buy it, I did without. So I bought what I could: an eighth of a kilo. Came about the size of a tennis ball, but hard like rock. I chopped it up and put it in those teenie-weenie plastic bags—twelve-twelves and ten-tens, which is millimeters by millimeters, plastic bags the size of postage stamps. Right away people knew I had Fish Scale, and even though it was so pure, I sold it for the same price as everybody else's. That's how you do: Take care of your crackheads, and you make them loyal to you. Man, in no time, we took that strip over. Those uptown niggers couldn't figure it out. I'll tell you though: If we'd tried that shit on North Capitol, they'd have shot our ass up. Lucky for us, them up on Georgia Avenue was weak niggers.

to understand why nothing had happened. The explanation was a chilling but defining moment for me. "Throughout the whole thing, the whole hundred days the massacres were going on," Steinberg said, "the White House *didn't get a single letter or phone call about it from a constituent!* There were many of us inside government who wanted to take more robust actions. But whenever we sought to do these things, those who opposed them would say that the American people would never support them, especially so soon after our Black Hawks went down in Somalia."

I could see that Steinberg was as upset about it as I was, if not more. After all, he was the expert on Africa for the president of the United States, and one of the worst genocides since the Nazis had happened on his watch. He dropped his hands to his sides and sagged his shoulders. "The fact that we couldn't point to cries for action, not just from voters but from Congress and the media, was damning to our case, and we lost out to those calling for inaction and to the forces of inertia. We were looking for a chorus of support that never showed up. We're a government of the people, by the people, and for the people, remember?" he said softly. "How do you expect the U.S. government to respond if there's no political constituency?"

I left his office a changed man. A new light bulb had lit up above my head, flashing neon: It wasn't going to be enough for me to learn about Africa and then convince the powerful. If American policy toward Africa was going to change, it was going to have to come from the people themselves. It sounds cynical, that many politicians will act only if they think it will win them votes or at least praise. And most of them surely wouldn't act on an issue like this if it would bring them nothing but condemnation and recrimination. But that's part of what representative democracy is, right? Why should we expect that policies regarding genocide would be made any differently than policies regarding health care reform? In theory, it should be easier to influence the debate on genocide than on health care reform because there presumably wouldn't be any big lobbyist firms working in support of genocide. So the task was clear: help build a political constituency for peacemaking in Africa, and against genocide and other terrible human rights crimes.

12. "Nonstop for the Ninjas"

MICHAEL MATTOCKS

We didn't realize how fast our crack business was going to grow. From day one it was nonstop for the Ninjas, which was the name of the gang me and James started up on Georgia Avenue. I was the president, and James was the enforcer. My man Fats couldn't keep up. I'd call and say I needed more, and he'd say he didn't have it, so I had to go up the chain to the man who did. I can't tell you his name because when he got locked up, a lot of motherfuckers got locked up with him, so I don't want to mess with that.

But he was a good dude. I'd call him up and say, "I need a loaf of bread." Or, "I need half a loaf." I'd call him every week without fail. He'd pull up in front of my mom's house and come inside. We'd never talk. He'd put the crack on the table, and I'd give him a bag of cash. Half a ki was like $10,000; the price never changed for me. And it was always good quality. He asked me once how I was pumping all that crack. He thought I was working with the police. I said, "One day you're not doing anything, you come chill with me, and I'll show you what we're doing. This block pumps." He did that, and he was like, "*Damn.*" After that, knowing I was such a good outlet for his crack, I'd give him his $10,000, and he'd give me back $3,000. He'd say, "This is all I want for it." Like I say, he was a good dude. It bothered me when he got caught. He's gone for thirty years, and I'm still out here. I think about that sometimes. I am a blessed man.

I'd take that half a ki and break it up and make $30,000, $40,000 off it. About three months after we started on Georgia Avenue, I counted my money. I had $28,000 in cold hard cash. I counted it three times, then counted it the next day. I was happy as a motherfucker. I was all about the money.

At first Nikki used to say, "Michael, you need to stop selling them drugs. You need to get a job." She was going to school, and working, and she didn't want any part of the life; it's not how she was raised. And I'd be, like, "Fuck, you know I'm going to sell my drugs. I'm going to take care of my family." But what I did was hide it from her. She never saw the guns around the apartment we shared in Northeast. I had so many guns—a big Army Beretta nine-millimeter, two four-fives, the MAC-10, a sixteen-gauge shotgun, and a .223 sniper rifle I bought from a white guy. I'd keep them around at different places. She never saw the drugs around our apartment either, except for this one time when I brought home half a ki of coke and, having no place else to hide it, stuck it in the oven. When I got home, the whole house smelled of the mac and cheese, ribs and greens that Nikki was cooking . . . and then I smelled something else. I ran to the oven, and $10,000 worth of crack cocaine was nothing but a big, black, bubbling mess. I let it dry and spent all night cutting it up, and only recovered about an eighth of a ki. That was some fucked-up shit. After that, I kept my drugs at my mom's.

The only thing I'd bring home to Nikki's was the money; I'd keep it in a big old garbage can. One day I get a page from Nikki, and I call her, and she's like, "We got to talk." I went home and she just lifted the lid on that garbage can; it was full of money—tens of thousands of dollars. So she knew what I was doing, but since she didn't see the drugs or the guns in her own house, she didn't beef with me about it.

———————

One day me and James, Sabrina, and David were down paying the phone bill at this little cash joint, and this guy says, "Look at these niggers."

That's all it takes. People think the shooting and the killing in the city is all about drug turf and drug deals. But most of the time it's just this: One guy eyefucks another guy the wrong way. Or says something. One way or another, one guy shows another disrespect, and then it's on. James is like, "What are you looking at?" and pulls out his nine. The guy just laughs. He was cool, I'll give him that. Says, "You pull a gun on me and there's a police right over there." Well James, he don't give a shit. He waits for the guy to leave and circles around to the end of the alley, and when the guy comes rolling down with a bunch of boys in a station wagon, James busts off seven or eight shots at the car, and they take off.

Couple days later, I'm inside my mom's house cutting up my shit, and I hear James. He's yelling. Yelling, "Nigger, I am going to *kill* your fucking ass!" That nigger from the store had come 'round to solve his problem, but you weren't going to solve no problem with James. I went out and grabbed him and said, "James, look around you. You got all these little kids around here." James goes off on *me!* He's like, "Motherfucker, I'm tired of you saving those niggers' lives and telling me what to do!" I thought he was going to put one in me! He finally goes in the house, and I go over and talk to those dudes, trying to be

Lots and lots of shooting, and here comes James, running back with this big old smile on his face, yelling, "I fucked them niggers *up!*"

The police pretty much left us alone, but that time they came round and were actually pretty nice about it. They explained that there'd been too many complaints, and that if somebody got killed, they were going to lock up the lot of us for murder.

I loved James, but there were times when he even scared *me*. Something in him just went off. It became a little bit of a problem in the neighborhood, actually. Niggers used to come to me and say, "Your brother is shooting at us too much," and I'd have to tell him, "Man, you can't do that shit." It was nonstop.

I'd get drawn in, because he was my little brother. One time, this dude named Money was trying to shoot James. Luckily, Money's three middle fingers was gone, and he couldn't get the little stub onto the trigger. I don't even know why James was beefing with this dude, but I couldn't have him trying to bust one in my brother. So I got Sabrina's .357—she loved that gun—and shot it at Money six times. I was on one corner of a side street right off Georgia Avenue, and he was diagonally across on the other. Man, a .357 Magnum is a loud goddamned gun. *BOOM! BOOM! BOOM! BOOM! BOOM! BOOM!* Lit that whole street up. I wasn't really trying to kill Money; I was just talking to him. I wanted him to know James had a brother, and that we had the power. He left James the fuck alone after that, I can tell you. Somebody shoots a .357 Magnum at you six times from like thirty feet away, you know you've been shot at.

I could never get over that though; I brought him into the life, and all his darkness found a way out.

all, "What's happening?" They were such gangs̲
minutes I had them apologizing.

But James, man. I learned to be real sorry I goṯ
with guns because he took too much of a liking tọ
he got in a beef over our sister Elsie. Elsie was tom-
she would get in fights, but it's not like she could
out for herself on those streets. She was only twelve,
was no Sabrina. She didn't smoke or drink, and sure diḍ
no .357 Magnum. When we were on Georgia Avenue,
going to school and to church with my mom on weekenḍ

So Elsie, she came along crying to James that some
Double-O niggers had hit her. They're the niggers from
500 block of Georgia Avenue. James and Elsie were real clọ
this was all he had to hear to get that creepy little smile on ḥ
face. James gets in the car and tries to run them all over, anḍ
puts his car into a pole. Gets out with the Club, the car lock,
and beats the shit out of a couple of them. But even that ain't
enough, and he runs home, gets his .380 and a bike, rides back
and peels off a few at them. Hits one of them in the arm. And
this is in broad daylight.

The uptown niggers would try to cut into what we were
doing. Or they'd want us to sell to them. One day they started
some shit, and James took the seat off his bike and beat three of
them half to death with it. That set off two days of gunfights.
First they shot up the back of my mom's house. Then James went
over by their corner with two guns and shot the place to pieces
but didn't hit anybody. Then they tried to kill a friend of ours
while he was in his car with his wife, and they put so many bullets
all over that car I don't know how nobody got killed that time.
Then James goes over a second time, and from where I was, it
sounded like a damned war. *Bam-bam-bam-bam-bam-bam-bam!*

JOHN PRENDERGAST

At some point I had to venture out and speak in public. I had emerged as a socially shy young man, after spending my formative years trying to be invisible. I was therefore petrified of the idea of talking in front of an audience. My first talk was on a panel at a Michigan State University conference, and a very senior academic in the audience tore my argument to shreds. It was humiliating, but it helped prepare me for much worse in later years. My second talk was a speech at a little conference in Chicago. Jean came with me, and she told me afterward I was visibly shaking with nerves, but that I did well and got my points across. I felt such relief, and I started to see the potential for these opportunities to communicate ideas to audiences who really wanted to learn and to do something to help.

It wasn't going to be enough, I now knew, for senators and representatives to hear about Africa from people like me on Capitol Hill in D.C.; they were going to have to hear about it from voters. They were going to have to believe that a significant subset of their constituents wanted them to do the right thing for Africa and would hold them to account. So in addition to traveling to Africa and lobbying members of Congress, I also would occasionally do talks around the U.S., to colleges, churches, conferences—whoever would have me. I'm sure I wasn't very good at it. But then again, I had some pretty compelling material to work with. I'd seen, with my own eyes, the starvation in Ethiopia, the anarchic mayhem in Somalia, the child soldiers in Uganda, the slave raiding in Sudan, and the genocide in Rwanda.

In 1996, I was invited to be part of a conference at Princeton

University. Just after I made my remarks, someone whispered in my ear that Susan Rice was in the audience.

Susan Rice? She was President Clinton's White House Senior Director for Africa. I'd just delivered a blistering attack on the Clinton administration for doing nothing during the Rwanda genocide, and for its deadly miscalculations in Somalia. I had just delivered my message directly to America's top Africa official, and I hadn't even known it at the time.

After the conference, I took a cab to the Princeton Amtrak station for the trip back to Washington. I was settling into my seat, hoisting a thick folder of reports onto my lap, when I saw Susan coming down the aisle with my friend Ted "the Emperor" Dagne, an Africa expert on Capitol Hill. The three of us ended up discussing and debating U.S. policy all the way down to D.C. I sensed in Susan a kindred spirit, someone who was totally committed to a better future for the people of Africa. And she was on the inside, working furiously within the system to try and change the policies and attitudes necessary for that better future.

My more and more frequent travel to and work in Africa came at the expense of the time I could spend with the boys. Michael was nearly twenty by this time, and he was pretty much lost to me by now. James too. But I was still taking their fourteen-year-old brother David out, and occasionally the youngest brother, Tyrell. Mostly I was just sad when I thought about it; I missed Michael and James, but my Africa vocation was calling me with ever increasing intensity.

13. "All About the Money"

MICHAEL MATTOCKS

I was going real wrong. I had the respect, the power, and the money. I was like Wesley Snipes in *New Jack City*. Cold, man. Cold. I was making $3,000 a day Fridays and Saturdays, and almost that much the other days. A crackhead can't go a whole day without smoking crack, so sooner or later he's going to bring me his money. And you'd be surprised at some of the people I was selling to. Sure, some were lowlifes, like this dude named Shitbag. He had a colostomy bag from the time he was fucked up on PCP and thought there was something crawling around inside him. He stuck a stick up his ass and tore himself all apart in there. Shitbag was a good dude. He got a veteran's check every month—he was probably around fifty years old—and had money, and he came to see me every day. But so did accountants, and dentists, and lawyers. I even had a musician from the Kennedy Center. All of them were black; I didn't like selling to white people because I didn't know who was an undercover agent. A lot of these people had money. Like, I mean, *money.* I'd serve some of these people at the window of their BMWs.

I'd get an eighth every three days, and I'd make about $3,000 off of that. I was good. Instead of giving people two for twenty,

I'd give three. Instead of three for twenty-five, I'd give four. So people would come looking for me. There were days I'd be selling so much drugs I'd actually get scared. We started selling dubs—double the amount in each bag—to reduce the traffic. And damn, it produced *more* traffic.

I used to feel like I was on top of the world. I got to be like John Gotti in that neighborhood. It got to where people would come to me with problems that weren't drug related. I'd lend people money for no interest. I'd give people a few dollars here and there when they were in a spot. I paid my mom's bills, and I bought clothes for my little brothers and sisters. I got my people to shovel the snow, rake up the leaves, keep the street clean. And there ain't nobody robbing or grabbing no purses on my blocks. I was the godfather up there, man.

———————

So I'm looking after James, and my mom, and my other brothers and sisters. I'm looking out for the old lady who lives up the block and the couple with the little kid who lives the other way. I'm looking after my violinist crackhead and my dentist crackhead and all my buddies who are selling for me and watching my back. I'm looking out for the neighborhood, making sure the leaves are raked and the snow is shoveled and the garbage is picked up. I'm even looking out for Shitbag. The one person I wasn't looking out for was the one person who I should have been putting all my heart into, and that was Nikki. There were times when she'd ask me for money, for something simple. And for no reason at all, I'd get stingy with her. Me, who'd peel off a ten for any crackhead on the street that needed something to eat. Nikki would ask me for $100 for something simple—some shoes, or a haircut—and I'd say, "What the fuck you want? We got everything!" I had an asshole full of money; I could have bought her the damn world. But I wouldn't do it, and I still don't know why.

Once on her birthday, me and her were supposed to be going out. She was working then with disabled people—hard, hard work—and she'd been looking forward all week to us going out. She's all dressed up fine, and she's like, "Michael, you ready?" And I said, "Look here, I got to wait for a guy to bring me $200. You go ahead, and I'll catch up with y'all." She went out with her sister, and I never did go meet her. I was cold, man. Ice cold.

All this time, J.P. would come and pick up my brother David, who was about thirteen, and Tyrell sometimes, and they'd go a bunch of places. When I was at my mom's, I would duck out when J.P. showed up; I didn't want him to see me. I didn't want to be judged. I'd run around the back of the house and up the alley, half expecting J.P. to come find me, but he never did. He'd put David and Tyrell in the car, and off they'd go.

I used to wonder if J.P. felt guilty about me in those days. I expect he did.

John Prendergast

I was already spending precious little time with the boys, but then it suddenly got a whole lot more challenging to steal even a few hours here and there with them.

My big break came when the U.S. Institute for Peace and

my friend there David Smock created in 1996 an unusual fellowship. They wanted to place a peace activist or researcher in a federal government executive branch office that didn't have the budget for another person. The institute would pay the salary for six months, and it had the clout and connections to get the person placed. There was only one opening, and I got the spot.

I knew immediately where I wanted to work: alongside Susan Rice. She had me into her office—in the building right next to the White House—for an interview. I admit it; I was a little bit intimidated. The walls and floors there practically vibrate with power. I passed through the security checkpoint, feeling as though I was approaching the summit of Mount Olympus. Finally, my visitor ID hanging around my neck like a cow bell, I found Susan in her office at the National Security Council.

She fixed me with that same level stare she'd used on the train and began firing questions about Africa at me. What did I think the prospects were for a peace agreement in Zaire? (Possible, but would take a lot deeper involvement in peacemaking.) What did I think of the effectiveness of the United Nations in Africa? (The United Nations is one of the most troubled organizations I've ever seen, and yet it is absolutely essential if we are going to solve some of the world's biggest problems.) What should we do about Somalia? (Start at ground zero and help rebuild a government from the bottom up, involving the people in each region and sidelining the warlords.) Her questions were pointed and detailed and very well informed. She listened intently as I answered, and I could almost see the pistons firing between her ears.

As we were wrapping up, she said she had one more question: Is the government of Sudan incorrigible?

A strange tension crackled between us. I knew the "correct" answer. In international diplomacy, conventional wisdom holds that no government is beyond hope. In hard political terms, you have to deal with the government of the day, no matter how heinous, and work to reform it. In the era of the nation-state, governments recognize and work with other governments. That is the reality. But in this case, the Sudanese government had been responsible for nearly 2 million deaths in the south of that country, and it hadn't yet perpetrated the genocide in Darfur. Despite all that, "incorrigible" might well be a forbidden word among diplomats. Sitting there in the Old Executive Office Building, with the White House right there out the window, I knew what I was supposed to say: Not at all. We can explore a number of avenues of influence, and we can help reform that government or modify its behavior, blah blah blah.

Instead, I heard myself saying, "Absolutely. The government of Sudan is incorrigible, and it ought to be changed before another million people die. Too deformed to be reformed."

Susan nodded. I couldn't read her face at all. She stood, I stood, we shook hands, and I made my way back out onto Pennsylvania Avenue.

The White House called that night: I had the job.

14. "Because I Know You Are Going to Change"

MICHAEL MATTOCKS

We weren't seeing a whole lot of J.P. He was in Africa most of the time, and then he got some big-ass job in government and worked all hours. But he'd show up out of nowhere at my mom's house from time to time and take David and Tyrell with him. I'd still hide sometimes when he came, so he wouldn't see me. Other times I'd be out when he came by, and I'd be pissed that I missed him. I didn't know what I wanted from J.P. I loved the life I was living, but on some secret level I wished for J.P. to reach down and lift me out of it. He was our big brother and our father all rolled in one, and I know he wanted better for me, even if he didn't say it.

Aside from J.P., the only real role model I had was Nikki's father, Cleo. He had what I always wanted; I just didn't know how to get there. On one level, I wanted the drug-dealing money to build a life and a family. But I think I always knew, on another level, that drug-dealing money wasn't real money—wasn't life-building money. It's flash money, play money, women-and-cars money. It's not the kind of money you can raise children on. It's funny how a hundred-dollar bill, earned one way, can do things that the same hundred-dollar bill can't do if you get it another way. In any case, I didn't spend a lot of time with Nikki's father after that first long talk. He didn't approve of what I was doing, even though he appreciated that I loved his daughter. But I'd see him from time to time, and it meant a lot to me that he was out there, that he was part of my world.

Me and Nikki got into a big motherfucking argument one day; I can't even remember what it was about. She jumped in the car and roared off, and I'm like, good, then go. Little while later, her cousin Clock calls me. "Where's Nikki?" he says.

"I don't give a fuck," I say. Mr. Big Shot. Mr. Tough Guy.

"You need to find her, Michael," Clock says. "You need to find her right now."

"What she needs to do is find *me*," I say. "She's the one needs to do the apologizing and the crawling."

"Michael," Clock says, and I can hear he's choking up. "Nikki's father just got killed. I mean it man. Shot down in the street. You got to find her."

I went cold all over. The one person in my life, besides J.P., who had nothing at all to do with the life—who didn't sell drugs, didn't take drugs, didn't profit in any way from the drugs—and he's the one who catches a bullet? The man I was holding up as the way a black man can live in this world? I couldn't believe it. Clock said Cleo had been walking home from church—from church!—and stopped at a grocery store for something. Two guys outside were beefing about something, one of them ran up an alley, and when he came back, he had him an AK. Way Clock told it, the dude cut loose from across the street and shot up everybody who happened to be near the guy he wanted to kill. Cleo walked out the store at that moment, caught a bullet in the throat, and died right there.

I got in my car and started driving around looking for Nikki. All the shooting I'd done, I'd never hit anybody except for the time I put two in my cousin Glen's leg when he was choking me out. That time I shot that .357 at Boo, all that shooting we did on North Capitol. . . . I never knew where all those bullets went when they left my gun. The important thing was to shoot, to make that flash and boom and see those other motherfuckers duck and run. But the bullets—I never thought about the bullets before, or where they come down. I remember J.P. telling James and me once that in some African country—Somalia I think—the militia dudes called their bullets "To Whom It May Concern."

I was driving past Takoma School, and I spotted someone kneeling in the middle of the playground. It was Nikki. Somebody had already told her about her dad, and she was crying so hard out there, alone, she was about to make herself sick. I took her to her parents' house, and then I acted like a real asshole; I didn't go inside with her. I dropped her there, and she went off to the hospital with her sisters. I went back to the street. Then came the funeral, and instead of standing beside Nikki and being a source of strength and help for her, I played Mr. Kingpin. I came in all stiff and proud, with my guys behind me, leaned over the coffin to look inside, sat down for five minutes like everybody was going to kiss my goddamn ring, and then got up and left. Instead of comforting Nikki, I'm back out on the street selling my drugs.

I don't know why I acted that way. I was so drunk on the respect I'd earned on those streets that I thought if I wasn't watching out for my interests out there, I could lose all that. I was like a celebrity in my neighborhood. I loved the respect I got up there. I thought I always had to be on my block in order to maintain control. But I wasn't taking care of Nikki. I don't know why she didn't leave me then. I asked her once, and all she said was: "Because I know you are going to change."

JOHN PRENDERGAST

I draped my brand new White House credential around my neck and passed through the doors of the Old Executive Office Building on my first day of work. I'd hoped to become some anonymous State Department desk officer by the time I was fifty, and here I was working on the White House staff at age thirty-three. I could scarcely believe it. Every night for the first couple months I worked there, my buddy and colleague Shawn McCormick and I would leave the office together late at night, and we'd walk across the front driveway of the White House, twenty feet from the front door. We'd just stop for a minute and stare reverentially at that symbol of so many things. The ever-present guy with the machine gun in his duffel bag, the Secret Service agent, eventually relaxed as he got used to our nightly ritual.

Anthony Lake was just ending his tenure as the national security advisor as I was coming on, and Sandy Berger was coming in to succeed him. I'd had the idea that I'd be a faceless drone in a windowless basement cubicle, churning out unread reports and hardly ever seeing Susan, let alone the national security advisor or the president. But instead I was right in the thick of things. The White House staff was small enough that you could play ball right away and be part of a team. Both Tony Lake and Sandy Berger were extremely sharp, passionately engaged, and surprisingly well informed on Africa. And both wanted to know more and more about the big African war zones: Congo, Somalia, and Sudan. It was never said, but I got the distinct feeling that the shadow of the 1994 Rwandan genocide was hanging over a number of people at the White House. It had happened on their watch, and they not only didn't want to let it happen again but perhaps they wanted somehow to make amends.

My six-month tenure was over before I could blink, and I was crestfallen at the thought of having to leave the White House just when I was starting to figure it out. Fortunately for me, Susan turned out to be brilliant not only when it came to international relations but also in navigating bureaucracies. I don't know how she did it, but she found enough space in the White House budget to give me a permanent position, with the grand title "Director for African Affairs at the National Security Council."

In my entire life, I probably hadn't spent more than $500 on clothes—cumulatively. After the rapprochement brokered by Jean, my father and I would go and buy suits at thrift stores and compete to see who could spend less. Cheap! We once got a couple of nice ones at a thrift shop for five bucks, brought in by some undertaker. That was one time I didn't want to ask any questions. Most of the suits I wore to the White House every day were thrift-store specials. Shawn used to feel the material of my suit between his fingers at the beginning of our staff meetings, then walk over to the blue institutional curtains, feel those, and then just shake his head in mock disgust and murmur, "Johnnie, Johnnie, Johnnie," as if my suits were made out of the same material as the curtains. Susan would double over laughing. She pestered me constantly to dress better. "Johnnie P, my brotherrrr, what were you *thinking* this morning?" She also pressed me to get a haircut, since although I had made concessions to the government lifestyle, my hair was still much longer than that of my other colleagues. Even the national security advisor needled me to get a haircut. After all, we were working for the president of the United States.

Amazingly, we really *were* working for the president of the United States. Bill Clinton didn't exist far above us in some murky firmament; he was our immediate boss. We wrote memos to him regularly, and they'd come back with his own handwritten notations in the margins: *Can we do more here?* Or: *What can I do now to help?* We frequently got chances to meet with President Clinton in the Oval Office. I'd go with Susan, and later with Ambassador Joe Wilson and then Gayle Smith, who replaced Susan when she went to the State Department. President Clinton exuded a palpable hunger to do right by Africa. He got few domestic political points for his deep and abiding interest, and yet he was constantly looking for a role or angle for the United States in problem solving. That mentality seemed to be part of his DNA: How could America's wealth, prestige, might, and creativity be deployed in support of solutions? Plus, it was clear he was playing catch-up. After his administration was hurt by what had transpired in Rwanda and Somalia, it seemed to me he may have felt he had a lot to make up for and little time.

Briefing President Clinton was a good lesson for me in the limits of power that even the president of the United States feels. He's not a king, after all. And sometimes other voices in the system—Congress, cabinet officials, to say nothing of the other countries in the United Nations—were arrayed against action. A common argument was: If we put our prestige on the line and fail, it will weaken us. I guess President Clinton agreed that that argument didn't apply universally; the consequences for the people of Africa if we did nothing were infinitely more severe, as Rwanda demonstrated. He probably had more briefings about Africa than any president that preceded him. Rarely, though, did President Clinton simply sit and listen. Sometimes he'd be reading a report while someone would be talking. Many times, I thought we'd lost him, that he was merely being polite, letting us drone on about Africa in his presence, and that his mind was a million miles away. But then suddenly he'd look up, with his reading glasses halfway down his nose, and ask, "What do you mean by that? Two minutes ago you implied something completely different." He caught people off guard more than once that way. His mind was so active; he just needed to exercise it constantly, I guess. Spending time around Bill Clinton really sharpened one's game.

Meanwhile, the youngest little brother, Tyrell, wasn't really coming with us too much, as he didn't have much of an interest in playing ball. The time I was spending now with David was focused on sports more than games or fishing. We would mostly play football and basketball, and I marveled at David's development as an athlete. He had the chance to be a special ballplayer. If I just would have spent more time with him, perhaps . . .

I hardly ever saw James anymore. He seemed to sleep most days away. Michael was around his mom's house a lot when he wasn't with Nikki, but he had become very withdrawn when I showed up, too cool to even acknowledge all the history we shared. I often wanted to really talk with him, but I honestly didn't know where to begin. So much time had gone by and so many things had happened, the gulf between us that had emerged seemed insurmountable.

Looking back, at first I simply didn't want to know what he was doing. Later, I was in denial about it all, once it became overwhelmingly obvious what Michael was into. But as time went on and I had opportunities to intervene, I chose not to get more deeply involved because of time constraints and other priorities. I simply let Michael down. And I couldn't even talk to him man to man. My dad had never once discussed anything important with me in my life after I was eight, and I repeated that pattern with Michael.

15. "Success Is Failure Turned Inside Out"

MICHAEL MATTOCKS

I was sitting on the porch of the Georgia Avenue house, look-ing across at Walter Reed, when J.P. pulled up to take David and Tyrell off to play basketball. They were really J.P.'s little brothers now. It was almost like they were from another fam-ily from me and James and Sabrina; they were a long way from the life. David was all about basketball; a lot of us thought he might really be headed for the NBA some day. He kept him-self away from drugs and drinking and all like that. Tyrell, he was only twelve. A funny kid—very sweet natured and gen-tle. Almost feminine. It was like the meanness of those streets couldn't touch Tyrell. I was glad he was getting his share of the J.P. thing—that relief from the stress of the lives we'd been born into.

David and Tyrell weren't around just then, or they were get-ting ready inside to go, so J.P. and I had a few minutes together on the porch. He looked good—not like a college kid anymore, but a grownup man with a nice suit, a beard, and long Jesus-style hair. We sat there, and I had a moment of wonder. This man had been in my life about fourteen years. He'd played a bigger role in my upbringing than my own father, or than the men my mom had lived with—Willie, Don, Kenny. Yet there was a big hole between us, a big gap neither of us could fill with words. It couldn't have been true that he didn't know what I'd become. Yet we pretended either that I wasn't a big-ass drug dealer or that he didn't know I was. I kept waiting for him to say, "Michael, you've got to give this up." I was even planning, in my mind, what I'd say when he said it. But he never did. He talked a little about working in the White House, and we made some kind of bullshit small talk. Then David and Tyrell came out the door and they were gone.

I'd gotten so powerful on my block, and I'd started to think I couldn't get caught, that the police lived in some other dimension and couldn't touch me. I even had my own police officer. This dude pulled up on me one day and said, "Here's how it is: You give me $100 every time I pass by, and I'll come holler at you when the police are coming 'round." A hundred dollars was cheap; I peeled one Franklin off for him right there, and sure enough, from time to time he'd cruise by and call, "Coming!" out the window, giving me just enough time to stash whatever gun or drugs or cash I had on me.

I was careful. But no matter how careful you are, you can't control the people around you. I come out the Chinese carryout one night, and out jump two guys with ski masks over their faces. They put me against the car, and I managed to take the cash I had and shove it down the crack between the fender and the hood so they wouldn't find it in my pocket. If they had, they'd have known I had crack on me too, and they would have taken me apart to find it. They pushed me rough into the back of a car, and I was yelling, saying, "Don't kill me, don't kill me," and they just laughed and pulled off their masks. They were cops. I'd served this lady, and she'd turned around and sold it to somebody else with the cops watching the whole time.

"Where's the shit, Mr. Mattocks?" they said, and like a good drug dealer, I said, "What shit?" The white cop slapped me across the face and said, "Give it to me or I'm getting out the rubber glove." I figured, fuck. "You got me," I said, reaching into my pants. My crack cocaine—about seventy-five rocks—was up under my nutsack. I handed it over, and they took me downtown.

This was too big a beef for any court-appointed lawyer, and I had buckets of money, so I got me a paid attorney. He worked out a deal: Three years' probation and thirty days of boot camp. Easy, I thought. I can do thirty days of anything, and no thirty days of boot camp is even going to touch my ass.

They told me what to pack: fourteen pairs of underwear and socks. They told me to cut my hair off before I went, but fuck that; I didn't listen. They picked me up in a bus with about twenty other guys and took us up to Fort Meade in Laurel, Maryland, and I'm thinking, this is going to be like summer camp. As we pull in though, I look through the window, and waiting for us are three big buff dudes in Army uniforms—one white, one black, and one Chinese. They look mean.

Minute I step off the bus the white one gets right up in my face about my hair, screaming, "Are we going to have a problem with you?" I'm like, *Who the fuck you think you're talking to?* I'm ready to throw down, but I know if I punch this dude, I'm going to jail for real. First thing they do is cut off all our hair and mustaches, so all we got left is eyebrows. And then it starts. Push-ups. Sit-ups. Ten-mile runs. Make your bed with a wrinkle in it and they tear the whole thing apart and make you start again. Calisthenics all morning, then a run, then classroom—math, history, English. Make you read an hour, hour and a half. Then cut the grass, pick up trash, more exercise, more running. By the time the end of the day comes, you're ready to sleep. This goes on thirty days, with those big Army motherfuckers yelling in our faces every minute.

But here's the other side of it; they took good care of us. The food was real good, and lots of it. And they talked to us with respect, about man things—taking care of the family, saving money, getting ahead at a job, talking to children. They yelled at us all the time, but because they were talking to us at other times about how to be better men, and because they were feeding us so good, it felt like all that yelling wasn't just to be mean but for our own benefit. There were guys in there who were just toughing it out and were going to go right back to what they were doing the minute they got out. They were hardened motherfuckers that nobody was going to touch.

They made us memorize a poem, said we were going to recite it at our graduation. We hear that and we're all groaning, like, what are we? In fourth grade? Graduation? Who gives a fuck about that? But you drill that poem into your head, and pretty soon you start hearing the words. Went like this:

> *When things go wrong, as they sometimes will,*
> *When the road you're trudging seems all uphill,*
> *When the funds are low and the debts are high,*
> *And you want to smile, but you have to sigh,*
> *When care is pressing you down a bit,*
> *Rest, if you must, but don't you quit.*

Life is queer with its twists and turns,
As every one of us sometimes learns,
And many a failure turns about,
When he might have won had he stuck it out;
Don't give up though the pace seems slow—
You may succeed with another blow.

Often the goal is nearer than,
It seems to a faint and faltering man,
Often the struggler has given up,
When he might have captured the victor's cup,
And he learned too late when the night slipped down,
How close he was to the golden crown.

Success is failure turned inside out—
The silver tint of the clouds of doubt,
And you never can tell how close you are,
It may be near when it seems so far,
So stick to the fight when you're hardest hit—
It's when things seem worst that you must not quit.

Funny thing was, as we reach day twenty-seven, twenty-eight, I'm looking forward to graduation like I'm a little kid. I'm a different man now than when I went in. For one thing, I'm built now; I got muscles on my body I never knew I had. And all that man-talk, beaten into me with those runs and calisthenics, had found that soft spot in me, that side that wanted out of the life when I was hanging with Cool, the side that has kept me from shooting anybody but my cousin Glen, the side that Nikki always claimed to see. On graduation day, Nikki and my

mom showed up to support me, and I marched past them proud
as a motherfucker. I shouted out that poem like it was coming
straight out of my own heart. I felt like a new man.

JOHN PRENDERGAST

The longest trip Bill Clinton had taken as president was one
a team led by Susan Rice and Joe Wilson helped organize to
Africa. During the trip, I helped write the speech the president
would be delivering in Rwanda, which was tricky and fraught
with implications beyond just the words that would be spoken.
President Clinton wanted to acknowledge the failure of the
United States to stop the Rwandan genocide. At the same time,
the government lawyers knew that a president has to be careful
not to admit too much. There's international law to consider,
and the possibility of giving somebody room for a claim against
the United States. There's the chance that too abject an apology
will give America's adversaries in the United Nations ammunition for an embarrassing resolution. The president, getting carried away with a *mea culpa*, might lock the United States into a
policy it wouldn't want to carry out in the future. So as we wrote
the outlines of the speech, we felt all these countervailing cur-
rents, and every sentence needed to be inspected, debated, and
agreed to by consensus.

In the end though, Clinton delivered key parts of the speech
in his own words. As we stood in the tension-filled Rwandan
airport hangar, the Secret Service agents scanning the hills for
any sign of the possibility of incoming mortar rounds, Clinton

spoke from the heart: "We did not act quickly enough after the killing began," he said. "We should not have allowed the refugee camps to become safe havens for the killers. We did not immediately call these crimes by their rightful name: genocide." As familiar with President Clinton and the issue as I was, I still found myself choking up as I stood next to some of the Rwandan genocide survivors, many of whom had lost their whole families and everything but their lives. It was a powerful thing to hear him use the word "genocide" after all the deadly controversy back in 1994 when his administration was unwilling to use the word and to fulfill its obligations in international law to respond. And it's even more powerful to hear a president say that the United States screwed up, and that it would do better the next time.

I was spending most of my time in Africa at that juncture. I was traveling from one conflict zone to the next as an advisor to President Clinton's high-level peace envoys. We were negotiating with presidents, rebel leaders, militia commanders, and warlords, and we were trying to find peaceful solutions to some of the deadliest wars in the world since World War II. Susan Rice and her team were building serious momentum for broader, deeper U.S. engagement in Africa. And the president himself was willing to support these efforts with personal diplomacy. This was my chance to finally accomplish something tangible.

It wasn't in my nature to rest on my oars, but I owed it to Jean to take a vacation. We'd gotten through President Clinton's marathon visit to Africa. Some of the negotiations were at a delicate stage where everything needed to cook a while, particularly in Sudan, where we were trying to build a peace process to end the deadly north-south war after some 2 million conflict-related deaths. Everything that could be said had been said, and all sides needed some time to look inward and find a way forward. And it was a couple weeks after the American embassies had been bombed by al-Qaeda in Kenya and Tanzania, and our White House team had barely slept working on the response. I needed a week off.

Jean and I decided to go to Morocco. There was no way that I, the supposed superhero, the guy who had too much work to do with too little time, was going to go lie on a beach at some resort. Morocco was a good compromise—beautiful, dreamy, historic, but also a serious destination with much to teach. And of course, in Africa.

We really needed the vacation together. I'd been largely absent from her life—working until midnight most nights, and then disappearing on foreign trips. In my absence, she had continued to strengthen my emotional bridge back to my father. He and I were talking even more now. I'd even taken him out to dinner a couple of times, just the two of us. Each time, I had intended to revisit our past, to find a way to ask him: What happened to us when I was a kid? What was it about me that made you so angry? But I could never find the words to ask, and instead we'd talk about sports or his memories of the frozen foods business. But after two decades of not making eye contact, talking football with my father was a huge step forward. It was Jean who had made that possible. And she was my wife! I had been an absent husband over the years, so I really owed her some of my undivided attention and a nice voyage.

We were in Marrakech, and, having toured hard the day before, we were planning to enjoy a leisurely day. We slept late and padded downstairs to breakfast in our hotel slippers. Jean wanted to poke around the market, which sounded good to me. I was feeling myself relax a little—an unusual feeling. It was August 21, 1998.

A television hung on the wall of the coffee shop, with its sound off. I didn't notice it at first, but then I saw a couple of people standing under it, looking at something. A few more people joined them. On the screen was footage of some destroyed building, which looked as if it had been bombed. More people stood under the television now, maybe ten.

I jumped up and ran to the television. They were watching CNN International, and it said "Sudan" across the bottom. The images were of smoking rubble, people wailing, men waving their fists. An American cruise missile had flattened a building in Khartoum. The Sudanese said it was a pharmaceutical factory. The U.S. government said it was a chemical weapons plant belonging to an alleged associate of al-Qaeda, a man who had been implicated in the earlier bombings of our embassies in Kenya and Tanzania. To me, it looked like the wreckage of our infant Sudan peace process—months of work, literally blasted to pieces.

I vowed never to take another vacation again in my life.

16. "Let's Stop This"

MICHAEL MATTOCKS

Rolando—who we called Lando—was four years old when Nikki gave me the most wonderfulest thing in the world: a baby boy: Michael Marcel.

One night, Nikki came by Georgia Avenue at about ten o'clock to see if I wanted a ride to the little apartment we shared in Hyattsville, Maryland. She had little Lando in the backseat, and nine-month-old Mike in a car seat. Nikki was pregnant again, and they looked so pretty all together—my own family. But I was still being the tough guy, and I said to her, no, you go on. James will drive me home.

Less than an hour later, I see Nikki's car coming up Georgia Avenue fast, and I think, uh oh. Something bad's happened. I could see it in her face when she screeched to the curb. She jumps out, crying, and tells me what she's been through since I saw her.

She'd been walking from the car to the apartment with little Mike in her arms and Lando by her side, when a man asked her, did she know where such-and-such an apartment was. No, she said, and she kept walking. "Well then," the man said. "Where's your boyfriend?"

Nikki didn't know enough to be scared at that point. She just got her back up. "What you worrying about that?" she snapped, and then out came the gun.

"We're going up to your apartment," the dude said. Now Nikki, she's smart. She knows there's a policeman living on the third floor, so she starts leading him up there. But the dude's been watching us, and he knows we live on the second. He takes her in the apartment, makes her sit in the chair, and then he and his friend start tearing our place apart.

I'd been expecting something like this. I'd gotten in the habit, when I came home, of taking out my gun and holding it in my hand as I walked to the door. Even if I was holding little Mike, I'd have him in my left hand and that big Army Beretta nine-millimeter in my right. And I'd moved most of my cash to Nikki's mom's house.

These dudes found two pistols, half a ki of coke, and about $7,000, but they were moving so fast and were so fucking stupid that they missed another $15,000 and another half a ki that I'd hidden. So while it hurt, it wasn't enough of a robbery to put me out of business. They didn't hurt Nikki, little Mike, or Lando, but they scared them real bad. I didn't like that one bit. It made me wonder how much the life would end up costing me.

JOHN PRENDERGAST

Of all the crises in Africa, the war between Ethiopia and Eritrea was one of the bloodiest and most heartbreaking. Ethiopia and Eritrea were locked in a senseless conflict that between 1998 and 2000 had already killed about 100,000 people, which made it the deadliest war in the world during that period. Most of these were shooting deaths, soldiers on the battlefield; very few civilians were being caught in the crossfire. Still, their war had settled down into World War I–style trench warfare—horrific slaughter every day, with few appreciable gains by either side. Our fear was that Ethiopia, which on some parts of the border had a five-to-one advantage in soldiers, would suddenly mount an all-or-nothing offensive and push through Eritrea to the Red Sea. The killing would have been wholesale, civilians would be caught in the maelstrom, and Eritreans would mount another insurgency like the one they conducted from the 1960s until 1991, the very war that had brought my attention to Africa seemingly so long ago on that La-Z-Boy chair. This offensive would ensure decades more war and hundreds of thousands more deaths at a minimum.

President Clinton decided to help stop the war. He had met both heads of state, and he felt the United States could play a unique role in ending the conflict.

He asked Tony Lake, his former national security advisor, to be his special envoy to the region, and Tony did it for free—didn't take a dime to do the job. Old-school sense of service, like no one I had ever met before. The consensus of the diplomatic community and many in the United Nations was: Yeah, right. You might as well try to solve the Israeli-Palestinian question. Ethiopia and Eritrea were locked in a death struggle, and no outsiders would be able to affect the outcome.

Tony Lake, two colonels from the Pentagon, and I began shuttling between Asmara and Addis Ababa. Back in Washington, punctuated by strategic visits, the diplomatic strategy was mapped out by Susan Rice, Gayle Smith, and Joe Wilson, all working closely with President Clinton. As we went back and forth between the two heads of state, we could show each that we knew where their troops were. We knew where they were strong, and where they were weak. And while we would never give one side specific intelligence about the other, we'd tell them enough about their own positions—in tremendous detail—to impress upon them how much we knew about the overall battlefield. This eliminated 90 percent of the usual diplomatic posing and allowed us to get right down to the business of negotiating peace.

In between marathon negotiating sessions, Tony and I would play basketball or tennis against the colonels. Tony had twenty years or more on the rest of us, but he was a terrific athlete. During one tennis match in which I hurled yet another racket into the fence in self-disgust, Tony dubbed me the "Latrell Sprewell of the tennis world," after the former basketball star more legendary for his volatile temper than for his hoops prowess.

Peace negotiations require commitment, and Tony Lake had it. President Clinton stayed involved by telephone despite all the impeachment nonsense he was dealing with back in Washington. Or maybe he was taking refuge there.

Because I was in Africa all the time working on these peace processes, I was seeing the boys less and less frequently. Michael's life was largely a mystery to me, as was James's. I had met Nikki a few times, and I felt that Michael was very lucky to have such a strong and committed woman by his side. Even with the shadow surrounding Michael's daily life, there was a stability about him that did not exist with the other brothers. When I'd see Michael, he was always solid as a rock, guarded to the point of impassive, exuding a quiet confidence and determination, occasionally flashing that tongue-in-tooth grin that had melted me when he was a little kid.

17. "To Tell Her What I Got Out of, I'd Have to Tell Her What I Got Into"

MICHAEL MATTOCKS

Our second boy together was born fine and healthy. I wanted to name him "Ginino the Don Mattocks"; I liked those *God-father* films. But Nikki wasn't having no child with "the" in his name, so we compromised and named him Ginino Da'Don. We moved out to Silver Spring, Maryland, but I didn't tell anybody about that robbery at our home a few months back. It shook us both up, and we didn't want to face a repeat of that shit.

I had a woman and three little sons at home now, and what was all my drug dealing getting me? All I really had to show for it was a lot of cars. James and I bought every car we liked even a little bit; we must have had twenty or twenty-five parked all over the city. Sometimes we'd drive them. Mostly we just owned them—bought and traded them around like guns or baseball cards, just for something to do. Didn't register or insure them or nothing. That tells you how bored I was getting with the life; I couldn't think of anything better to do with all that money I was making. And even though we were living in Maryland, I was still going down to Georgia Avenue every day to take care of business.

One day James came to me and said, "Michael, I'm fucked up. I got no money."

Well, that was James. He never could hold onto it. I said, "How much do you need?" And he said, "Sixteen hundred dollars."

I peeled it off and gave it to him. Couple of days after that, I was out without any money in my pocket, and I turned to James, and I asked him to give me $200.

"I ain't got no money."

I stepped back and gave him a long hard look. "Nigger," I said, "I gave you $1,600 not two days ago."

He just shrugged. "I ain't got no money," he said, and I'm thinking: Shit. We're to the point where the money doesn't mean anything to us. We can't even keep track of it. James was still living with our mom. By this time he had three kids, so most of the money he was making went straight to them and their mom.

It was around then I started noticing that the police weren't hanging around us anymore. The cop I was paying wasn't cruising by, and the uniformed police seemed to be staying away. At the same time, there was a new crop of unmarked cars cruising around, driven by hard-faced men with curly little wires in their ears.

It came to me like a bolt of lightning: This life is over. I was twenty-two years old and had been dealing drugs for ten years. It had been a good run. I'd made a lot of money, earned a lot of respect. I hadn't killed anybody, and I hadn't done any serious jail time. But it was only a matter of time before somebody tried to rob me again, and the next time, either Nikki or me—or the boys—might get hurt.

It was time to get out.

"James," I said to him one Thursday. "We're going to sell off everything we got on Saturday night, and that's it. We're getting out of the life."

"What the fuck do you mean?" James said. James cou[ld]
see what I was seeing.

"The feds are onto us," I explained. "This is it. We're d[one.]
I'm not going to prison for no thirty years."

James made a face and walked away. Come that Saturd[ay,]
I sold it all off and went out to our home in Silver Spring.[I]
put the money I'd earned that night in the same trash can [I]
used to hide it in when we lived in our apartment, and I sa[t]
down on the couch, feeling weird, disconnected—like I'd just
left home all alone. Nikki came home from work, and I didn't
say anything about it. To tell her what I got out of, I'd have to
tell her what I got into. For some reason I didn't tell her I'd left
the life, even though it would have made her happy. I kept up
appearances—went out at night like I always did, but now I
just drove around, with no drugs or money in the car. I'd see the
police and tense up, but then I'd relax. They couldn't touch me
anymore.

JOHN PRENDERGAST

The negotiating to end the war between Ethiopia and Eritrea
went on for two years; that's how committed President Clinton
and Tony Lake were to finding peace. The climax came in Al-
giers. We'd somehow managed to talk the foreign ministers of
the two countries into staying with us in a sprawling, near-empty
presidential palace a stone's throw from the Mediterranean Sea.
The place was enormous, and there was nobody there for long
stretches of time but us four Americans, the two foreign ministers,

a brilliant and affable Algerian diplomat, Ahmed Ouyahia, who worked closely with Tony, and a tiny staff. I felt like Jack Nicholson in *The Shining*, wandering around the vast deserted hallways. We were there on and off for months—negotiating, wandering, negotiating. For me, the days and nights all started running together. I was out of place, out of time, cut off from the world, dizzy from all the long sessions.

An undiagnosed but deepening depression was enveloping me during this period. That hole in my heart that I'd felt since childhood was still there, and it seemed to be getting larger, not smaller. Whenever I felt its sting too acutely, I'd just bury myself in more work, hoping it would eventually recede and hoping for affirmation and redemption somehow in a job well done. But I was carrying a huge bowling ball of anxiety and sadness around wherever I went. True, I had a great job and a great life, but I had progressively walled myself off emotionally from everyone that mattered in my life, and I was drifting away from Jean. I painted a smile on my face every morning to mask the hurt. The accumulated trauma of a childhood spent at war with my dad and an adulthood spent working in war zones with the survivors of real wars had led me to construct a self-protective emotional prison, carefully calibrated to avoid intimacy and emotional risk. But the cracks were beginning to form in this artificial edifice.

Often, during my wanderings, I would think about Michael and James. I felt helpless and disconnected from them. The world I had inhabited had changed so much since when I first met them. The same could be said for Jean. How was it that I could help end wars in Africa but I couldn't help straighten out the lives of a couple boys in Washington, D.C., or my own marriage?

The stakes, meanwhile, were increasing daily. Ethiopia was massing its forces for a major offensive aimed at overrunning Eritrea all the way to its Red Sea coast right across from Saudi Arabia. Then, one day, after a couple of separate private sessions with the foreign ministers of the two countries, Tony came down the stairs with a piece of paper in his hand, a ceasefire agreement, and that was that. The guns went silent. The deadliest war in the world at that time was over.

The experience gave me a deep appreciation for the "soft power" of American diplomacy. Throughout much of Africa especially, there is an unstated and profound respect for the United States and all it represents. That we were never a colonial power in Africa probably helps. But well-motivated Americans also have a knack for making deals, for finding a way that serves all sides and keeps negotiations from becoming a zero-sum game.

The most important ingredient in this case, though, was a thoroughgoing allegiance to the very idea of diplomacy, to finding a solution through discussion and through addressing the core interests of the parties involved in the deadly dispute. It takes a long attention span and an appetite for hard, uncomfortable work. Our country can be very good at it when it wants to. But it has to want to.

18. My Father's Grandsons

MICHAEL MATTOCKS

Man, the days and nights are long when you're not hustling anymore. I'd get up late, hang out, drive around a little, go to the bars. But the passion for the drugs had left me, and I really had no desire to go back up to Georgia Avenue and take that all up again.

Sabrina's new boyfriend was a cop—a uniformed D.C. police officer we called Duke. He was pure cop—his father had been one too—but Duke was a real good dude. He knew what I'd been, knew about Sabrina and her .357, but he didn't judge us at all. He was a man of a man too. He'd put his big hand on my shoulder and say things like, "Michael, you got babies now. You got to get yourself a job and take care of them." And I'd listen to him! Me! Listening to a D.C. policeman in his uniform and gun belt! Duke would talk to me like the dad I never had, and because I'd left the streets, I was ready to listen to him.

But it's not like I went out and got myself a job. When I needed money, I reached into the trash can. I didn't even know how much I had in there; I'd never counted it. But it was an assload. Then it was half an assload. Then a quarter. I could see the money was running out, but couldn't rouse myself, somehow, to do anything about it. It was like being in a car accident where everything slows way down and you can watch the disaster happen. I knew I'd be broke soon, but couldn't make myself do something about it. If I'd been thinking, I could have taken that money and invested it—bought a business or some stocks and bonds or some shit. But on some level, I think I wanted to go completely broke. In my own way, I was looking for the bottom so I'd know where it was.

Every now and then, James would give me a few rocks so I could make some money. But it wasn't for the money or even for the thrill that I'd serve from time to time. It was mostly out of boredom. I'd taken drug dealing out of my life, and I hadn't found anything to replace it with.

Although I never told Nikki I'd stopped selling drugs, she could see I was around more and wasn't in the life. She was glad about that. At the same time, though, my responsibilities were growing, as I continued to pay my mom's bills, buy stuff for my brothers and sisters, and take care of my own boys. Times were tough, and we needed that money just to get all the bills paid.

And then one day, about a year after I stopped dealing, I reached in that trash can and it was empty. I felt like a building had fallen on top of me; I sat down on the couch and couldn't get up. I don't know why it hit me like such a surprise; I knew this day was coming. But now it was here. I was broke—as broke as my mom had been when we'd been staggering from shelter to shelter with those Hefty bags full of our shit. I'd been a king on Georgia Avenue, the Godfather, the man. And now I was nobody.

"Michael, what's wrong?" Nikki said to me, in that Nikki way that's both sympathetic and get-your-ass-up at the same time.

"Nothing."

"Don't tell me that," she said, putting her fists on her hips and just about setting me afire with that ferocious gaze of hers. "You ain't moved off that couch in two days. You just moping around. What is it?"

"Nothing," I said again, and then all the resistance in me drained away. "Nikki," I said. "I'm fucked up. I'm broke."

"What do you mean, you're broke?" she barked. She walked to the garbage can and swept the lid off it. "Where's all your money?"

"It's gone. It's what I'm telling you. I ain't hustling no more."

She stopped and gazed down at me with those big, hot eyes of hers. "Ain't hustling?" she yelled. "How we going to pay rent and shit?"

Then she stopped. She could hear what she was saying. She'd never liked me dealing drugs. But now she was admitting she'd become dependent on the money the drug dealing brought in. She walked out of the room, and she and I didn't talk all the rest of the day. But as we were getting into bed that night, she pulled me close and said, "I'm happy you're not dealing anymore. Don't worry about the money. We'll get by."

JOHN PRENDERGAST

My brother Luke and his wife Kim ended up having two sons, Dylan and Michael. Dylan is the older by two years. Dylan fell into a coma as a newborn as a result of an undiagnosed medical disorder, but he survived that rough beginning. As the boys got older, the three of us founded our own Good Samaritans' Club, in which our purpose was to look for nice things to do for other people. These were my brother's sons, flesh of my flesh, my father's grandsons. We were like three kids together as they grew up, and we all called Luke "Dad."

From the time they could talk and walk, I was almost freakishly close to both Michael and Dylan. But I had a special responsibility to Dylan, as I was his godfather. And I took the job seriously.

Dylan has some ongoing learning and motor challenges, and he couldn't quite get the hang of riding a bicycle, despite $75-an-hour therapy sessions. One wintery day Luke and I were out in the street in front of their house, taking our shot at teaching Dylan and Michael to ride a bike. Michael picked it up right away, as he does most things, but Dylan was having a harder go of it. Once he got going, he did just fine, but getting the start down was hard for him. After a while, we all got cold so Michael and Luke went inside. Dylan, though, wanted to keep at it. And despite my malaria-induced intolerance for cold weather, I hung in there with him. I remembered back to when I was his age, when I had severely pigeon-toed feet. One of our older neighbors in Kansas City, a cadet-in-training named Whit McCoskrie, took me under his wing and put me through a summer of painful physical therapy that almost completely straightened out my feet.

He ain't heavy, Father, . . .

So Dylan and I stood in the driveway trying over and over. Dylan never got too frustrated, never got too mad, just frowned each time and said, "Again." The shadows grew long. It started getting dark. It was very cold. Dylan, who was only eight, wouldn't give up. "Again," he said. "Again." Luke and Kim called to us from the window: Come on in. Dinner's ready. It's

J.P. and Dylan

getting dark. But Dylan wouldn't stop until he figured it out. Finally, after about six hours—both of us blue with cold—he got the left-foot/right-foot timing down, and he took off down the driveway on his own. It was so dark by then I couldn't see him turn around, but then here he came, grinning like mad, raising his arms and jumping like he was Rocky on the top of the Art Museum's steps. That's Dylan.

Out of the blue, I got a call from James. He'd gotten himself a job, and he asked Jean and me to come down and see him. I hadn't seen him in a while, and I wasn't seeing or hearing much from Michael either. Occasionally I'd get a call, and every once in a while I'd go out and make a quick visit to Michael and Nikki and the kids, but it was always hit-and-run, just saying hello. It hadn't worried me too much; James and Michael were grown up now, and what I was about was being a big brother to young boys. It never occurred to me that James and Michael might not have seen it that way. To them, we were no less brothers now than we'd been when we were fishing together on the dock behind the Watergate when they lived in the homeless shelter.

Now in his early twenties, James looked thin, but happy. He was wearing baggy pants and a tight, fashionable shirt. His hair was neatly braided. I'd never seen James at a job before. "I'm going back to church," he told us. "I've been going with my mom."

He alluded to having given up "the life," and Jean and I both told him how proud we were of him. It was easier to talk about "the life" with him now that he'd given it up than it was to deal with it while he was all in.

"I gotta take care of my kids," James told us. "I don't want them ending up doing what I been doing."

"How's that temper of yours?" I asked.

He smiled. "I got that under control now," he said softly, then chuckled. "I used it all up." He was very proud of his kids, and he seemed to be at peace for the first time in his life. Jean and I tried to be very encouraging about keeping on this track; we vowed to be in closer contact going forward.

He didn't have a very long break, and he had to get back to work where he was on a clean-up crew at a D.C. auditorium. We hugged and said goodbye. I started to feel as though maybe I should get a little more involved in supporting James' choices, resuming my big brother role to the extent he wanted or needed it.

Not long after that, Michael called. "J.P., I got to see you," he said, and my first thought was: This is his one phone call from jail, that he has finally done something really serious and needs me to get him out of it.

"Sure, buddy," I said. "What's going on?"

"We'll talk when I see you," he said. I drove out to his new apartment in Laurel, Maryland, and we sat on their couch set with Nikki, our knees practically touching. Michael looked shaken and tense, and I began wondering if he'd done something irretrievably serious.

"J.P.," he said. "I fucked up."

"Fucked up how?"

"I'm broke, man," he said, and I immediately felt a flood of relief. If it was only money, nothing serious was wrong at all. I realized that it was the first time money had ever come up between us. In all our years of being brothers, he'd never asked me for a nickel; it hadn't been a part of our relationship at all.

"What happened?"

He looked at Nikki, who nodded at him and nudged him with an elbow. "I been dealing drugs, J.P.," he said. "You know that, right?"

Did I know that? Of course I did. It had been the elephant in the room for a decade or more. It was strange to have it come up so plainly now, after all these years of denial by avoidance. The conversation was getting real in a way for which I had never really prepared.

"But here's the thing," Michael went on. "I stopped dealing cold a while back, and I'm out of money, man. I'm broke."

I breathed a little easier. I could get out of this conversation, maybe, by writing a check. He needed a little money, that's all it was.

"I started down on North Capitol Street," Michael went on.

"Wait. Started what on North Capitol?"

"Dealing."

"What, like pot?" My mind was locking up. Michael had been a little boy on North Capitol.

"Crack cocaine," he said, with exquisite precision, as though pinning me like a butterfly to a piece of cardboard. "I was a drug dealer, J.P."

"Like selling a little bit on the corner?"

He sighed and looked at the floor between his knees. Sitting there, holding Nikki's hand, the babies yelling from the other room, at twenty-three, he looked like the weight of the entire world was on his shoulders. As I stared at the corn rows on the top of his head, I thought: How did all this happen?

"I was a drug dealer, J.P. That's the size of it. I was a drug dealer. You don't really need to know it all. But that's what I was, and I ain't no more. I'm fucked up. I need help, J.P., is what I'm saying."

I took out my checkbook and wrote him a check. The sound of the pen point on the paper echoed through the room. I put it on the coffee table between us.

"I'm going to show you, J.P., that I can do it," he said, as he picked up the check, his eyes shining. "I want to make you proud of me. Tell Uncle Bud, tell Jean, tell your mom and dad, that I'm getting it together. You're all gonna be proud of me."

"We already are, buddy. You know you can always come to me and tell me anything." Even as I said it, I realized it was something I should have told him years earlier.

19. "You Don't Look Like J.P.'s Brother"

MICHAEL MATTOCKS

It was hard telling J.P. how bad I'd fucked up, and it was hard to ask him for help. I don't know why it was; it shouldn't have been. But I'd kept a lot from J.P. over the years, and I'd lied to him the few times the issue came up. And what hung between us was that conversation we should have had a million times but never did—the one where he said, Michael, this ain't right; you got to stop dealing them drugs. The one where he said, Come live with me again, this time for good. Because we'd never had that conversation—a conversation that for years I'd both dreaded and prayed for—it told me he didn't want to know about my real life as a grownup man.

Anybody with eyes in his head would have known I was a drug dealer. I walked like a drug dealer. I talked like a drug dealer. I dressed like a drug dealer. My mom told him a thousand times I was a drug dealer. Yet he barely mentioned it. That meant he didn't want to deal with it. So to tell him now that that's what I'd been doing all those years and was broke because I quit doing it, well, that hurt. I didn't tell him too much.

He wrote me a check, which got me out of my immediate hole, and he told me he'd find me a good job. Two days later,

J.P. called with the name of some dude he knew who owned a roofing company and was doing a big job at a housing development in Maryland. If I went over there, J.P. said, he'd put me on the work crew. But when I drove out there and introduced myself as J.P.'s brother, I could see right away we were going to have a problem. He looked me up and down like, You don't look like J.P.'s brother. The dude's wife was worse: She practically said, What the fuck are you doing here? They had all Spanish guys working, and they was underpaying every motherfucking one of them. He kept me on a couple of weeks to make it look good, and then the guy told me, "That's it. There's no more work." But I drove down there the next day and everybody was still working. Racist is what he was. I told J.P. about it, and it made me feel good that he was as pissed as I was. He said, "I will never speak to that dude again." And he never did.

We started seeing J.P. a little more. He'd come by and take us all to Fuddruckers or Buddy's. What blew my mind was, every place we'd go, someone would come up to J.P. and say, "Aren't you John Prendergast?" They'd be like, "I read what you wrote," or, "I saw you on TV." I had no idea what the fuck they were talking about. J.P. had told me he was working in the White House and in the State Department or some shit, and it was always about Africa. But until I saw strangers coming up to him to shake his hand, I had no idea he was such an important man. It made me proud to be his brother.

I couldn't keep touching him for money though, and after that racist shit with the roofer, I had no appetite for going out to look for work. Then an opportunity came up. Just like in the movies: One last job.

JOHN PRENDERGAST

Jean had always argued that whatever effect my friendship was having on Michael and James evaporated the minute I was out of their sight because of the environment in which they lived. And I'd always responded—more out of wishful thinking than anything else—that what I was trying to do was to plant a few seeds. By showing them that somebody loved them—that somebody cared whether they lived or died, succeeded or failed—I was keeping a lifeline open to them. Those meetings with James and Michael kind of proved both of us right. At one point, Jean actually said to me, "I see your point," and the funny thing was, I was about to say the same thing to her.

I'd let Michael and James down; there was no denying that. For almost a decade, I'd drifted in and out of their lives without ever engaging the deadly reality at their center. I'd figured all along that Michael was doing some nickel-and-dime drug dealing. But to hear the details—that he'd been a major player, that they'd regularly carried guns and used them—really shocked me. I didn't get it all in the first or second meeting. After that first confessional conversation at his apartment in Maryland, we slowly drifted back into each other's lives.

Eventually, the Bush II era began and my run in government service ended. I was back in the activist world. Now that I was out of government and couldn't help negotiate peace agreements myself, I decided to go back with renewed vigor to helping develop a popular constituency for peace in Africa, so that the next time genocide or famine reared up on the continent, the White House and Congress would be flooded with calls for meaningful action.

I was still busy, but at least my hours were a little bit more my own and I had more time for Michael. As we spent some evenings together, additional details about his life bubbled to the surface. The corrupt cops. The gunfights. The beatings. Each new anecdote acted on me at first like a drop of corrosive chemical, eating away my own shell of denial. I was amazed; it didn't seem possible that the James and Michael I had first known in the shelter could have done these things. I'd elected to see them only as the little boys I'd first known and loved.

The environment in which Michael had grown up was an undeniable factor, yet somehow I had divorced my assessment of Michael's prospects from the stark reality of his surroundings. Imagine how hard it is for boys like Michael to overcome the following context:

- One third of black males in their twenties are under some form of criminal justice supervision, and in cities like Michael's Washington, D.C., the number surges to over half.
- Less than half of African-American males graduate from high school on time, and a majority of the nongraduates will end up incarcerated by their thirties if current trends continue.
- A staggering 75 percent of people currently in prison on drug-related crimes are African American despite the fact that usage rates are roughly similar to those of white people.
- There are more African Americans who are incarcerated, on probation, or on parole than were enslaved right before the Civil War.

- People who commit violent crimes were themselves often subjected to terrible abuse and neglect when they were young and defenseless, and nothing was ever done about it.
- Children fall through the tattered "safety net" as they leave or are pushed out of segregated schools, are passed around in foster care, suffer abuse and trauma, enter the juvenile justice system, serve time for a felony, and eventually become de facto second-class citizens who face discrimination in their attempts to get employment, housing, and schooling.
- After doing so little for these young people as they are growing up and dealing with abuse and single parenthood, our government finally steps in and starts really spending money on these folks once they make a big mistake, to prosecute and put them away in prison for a long, long time.

These are the kind of things Michael and I would sometimes talk about, and we'd just shake our heads at how messed up things had become.

As I told Jean, she'd been right. My effect on them had been limited to the times I was actually in their presence. Just as she'd predicted, the overwhelming reality of their circumstances had taken over the minute I'd gone to Africa or anywhere else that wasn't with them.

Jean, though, saw something else. Yes, she said, the boys had gone off course for a while. But they'd pulled away from the brink. So many drug dealers end up either dead or in prison, but Michael had escaped and James seemed to have a chance as well. As far as we knew, they appeared to have stopped dealing and carrying guns of their own accord. And while we'd never know for sure, Jean argued, it seemed likely to her that one of my "seeds" had taken hold, just as I'd argued all along.

There is all kinds of evidence—both anecdotal and academic—that these big brother–big sister types of mentoring programs have a remarkable effect over time on kids' development, and countless school-based and community programs have been found to make a major difference in preventing crime and promoting achievement. They're just chronically underfunded, and desperately need more volunteers. Maybe Michael and James would have pulled themselves up and out of the violence and drug dealing if I had never been a part of their lives. But it's also possible that having someone care about them early in their lives had had the desired effect at just the crucial moment.

Of course, there was no way to be sure.

20. Strange License Plates

MICHAEL MATTOCKS

I was out of the life, but I still got the news. And the news was, there was a coke shortage in D.C. Nobody seemed to have any, for some reason, and the crackheads were getting fidgety. It's not good when the coke runs short. Prices go up. People get nervous. Bullets fly.

There was this guy I knew, no names necessary, who said he knew some dudes from Philadelphia who could bring in a full ki of coke. A kilo is a lot of crack cocaine; it's big money. I didn't have anywhere near that kind of money anymore; in fact, it was only because I was flat broke that I was even thinking about cocaine. James and I decided we wouldn't buy that ki of coke; we'd rob it.

It isn't easy getting a kilo of crack away from drug dealers. You need guns, you need brains, and you need big brass balls even to think about robbing them. I arranged to meet the Philly dudes at the McDonald's on New York Avenue. I took a soft-sided laptop bag and put a couple of folded towels in it, so if you felt it from the outside, it seemed like it was full of cash. I strapped up with two guns and James had two also; I'd left the life, but we still had guns. We met in the parking lot; six of those motherfuckers got out the car. I look up and see this extra dude on a fire escape, and I think, uh oh. He's with them too. But it was too late now to back out. I get James to keep most of them busy talking, and I say to the dude with the bag, let's walk around the corner and let me see the shit. It's all there, a full kilo of cocaine, and I feel my heart going like a motherfucker. I say let's go back to the car and get you your money. I hold out the laptop bag with my right hand and reach for the cocaine with my left. The dude puts his hand on the laptop bag, and I can see in his eyes he knows right away that isn't crinkly money in there, but cloth. He says, "Yo, yo, yo," and before he can do anything else, I drop the laptop bag and pull out my gun. "Ain't no use for *that*," he says and puts his hands up. I yelled to James, and we got in the car and went before any of those dudes could come unstuck. I never did know if the guy I saw on the fire escape was one of them. All I knew was, we'd just robbed some Philadelphia drug dealers of a kilo of crack cocaine and lived to tell about it. I sold it off cheap, and we still made $25,000.

After that, I was like, fuck that shit. I'm done. I knew it like God was talking in my ear. I was lucky one too many times. It had been more than a year since I'd left the street, and my half of the $25,000 wasn't going to keep us going very long with three little boys in the house.

So we all moved in with Nikki's mom. That hurt me; a man should be able to take care of his family. It was the most hurting-est thing I'd ever done. But I was stuck in the used-to-be and was waiting for the not-yet. It took me a while to figure out the rock-bottom truth: I had to get a job. A job. It stung even to think it. I'd never had a job except that roofing shit. Hardly anybody in my family had ever had a job. Nikki's sister said she could get me an interview at Washington Hospital Center and that I should go over and ask for a white man named Jeff.

This Jeff dude took one look at my cornrows and turned to the lady sitting there beside him. "Looks like a drug dealer," he said, and I almost went off on him. Like, what the fuck does a drug dealer look like anyway? I hadn't dealt any drugs in months.

"No," said the lady next to him. "I think we should give him a chance. What about it, hon? You want a job? You want to start right now?"

I said sure, and for the first time in my life, I was a working man. She put me in the cafeteria, washing tables to start. I felt all kinds of different ways all at once. Depressed, first of all; it's not any fun washing tables. Not like hanging on the corner with a big roll of bills and a four-five in my pocket. But also kind of calm and peaceful because I didn't have to be looking over my shoulder all the time for the thugs and the cops. And a little bit proud too. I was holding a job.

Of course, come that Friday and I get my paycheck, I was like, What the fuck is this? $423. I called up Nikki and said, "You know what this is? I wash tables all fucking week and make this? I used to make this in ten minutes dealing drugs!"

She was like a fucking rock though. "You got to stay with it," she told me in that voice that allowed no bullshit. And her mom was all over me with hugs and kisses and how proud she was that I was working an honest job. That woman loves me, and she loved me even more for putting on those overalls and going to work for no money. And J.P. was real proud of me too. They kept me at it.

I didn't tell them, but my plan was to save up four or five of those little paychecks, buy me an eighth of a ki, and do a little dealing on the side. I was going to outsmart all those motherfuckers. But a funny thing happened. By the time a few weeks went by, I was liking the work. Punch in. Say good morning to everybody. Do my work. Have lunch. Talk to people. Work some more. Punch out. I'd even see guys from the street in there, and they'd do a double-take and say, "What the fuck are you doing?"

"Working," I'd say, and I'd be proud. To find somebody else in my family who worked steady you'd have to go all the way back to slave times.

John Prendergast

My dad was laid off from Fred's Frozen Foods after nearly forty years as a traveling salesman. It was a blatant case of age discrimination, and the unfairness of it really burned me up. His professional life to which he had dedicated so much had come to a fairly abrupt and unceremonious end. Good old Fred's Frozen Foods had been sold and re-sold, and Dad was just an employee number to headquarters by then, not the guy who the secretaries would cheer when he and his partner, Uncle Dave, would come back to the plant in Indiana with a bunch of new sales, guaranteeing paychecks for everyone for the foreseeable future. He was the last of the dinosaurs, the older guys who relied purely on personal relations to make the sales. Traveling around in his station wagon with Uncle Dave for years, making friends, telling jokes, slinging product. To no longer do that made him feel unwanted, unneeded, it seemed to me. He suddenly lacked purpose and professional identity—a salesman without a customer.

One night when I was visiting the house in Berwyn, we watched Dustin Hoffman play the character of Willy Loman in Arthur Miller's *Death of a Salesman*. It was a remarkable distillation of the dreams and disappointments of a salesman's life, and to watch it with my father was powerful. To have Willy dream of hundreds of people at his funeral, "with their strange license plates," and then have nobody but his wife and sons at the graveside was painfully tragic. I glanced over at my dad, but he was impassive. When the play was over, a million questions ricocheted around the inside of my skull. Was that how he felt about things? Was that an accurate portrayal of the salesman's mentality? Did he feel as used up and spit out as Willy Loman did? "You can't eat the orange and throw the peel away," Willy had thundered. But my dad and I didn't have the vocabulary for that kind of talk. We just turned off the set and bade each other good night.

———————

A month or so after the September 11 attacks, Michael and Nikki were married. They'd reserved a big community center in Silver Spring, and there must have been 150 people there. Nikki was pregnant with Marco; they'd soon have four boys running around their feet.

It was like the final scene in a Fellini movie: Everybody from Michael's past was there. His brothers and sisters, of course, but also all his cousins and aunts and uncles who'd been drifting in and out of his life all those years, sponging off him and his mom when they could. His father was there. Tough-looking buddies from his drug-dealing days and straight-arrow folks from his job at the Washington Hospital Center. Michael had spent so much time and energy on building up and protecting his family. To see them all—the admirable and the not-so-admirable—all gathered around Michael and Nikki was a beautiful thing. And, in the middle of all that, my parents.

Michael's wedding really gave Dad a lift. He and Mom danced every dance. Michael kept finding them in the crowd and hugging them. He was so happy to show us that, after all the time on the streets, he really was the good soul we'd loved in him as a child. To have my parents at his wedding—to validate his goodness, to put their stamp on it—seemed really to overwhelm him. He had talked for years about the importance of family, and here he was showing us that he could live up to his words.

Michael and Nikki at their wedding, 2001

21. "I'll See You Tomorrow in Church"

MICHAEL MATTOCKS

James had really straightened himself out. He had four kids to look after now, and he was living with their mom and the kids. He had gotten himself trained to be a plumber. In the old days, I never saw James without a gun in his belt. Now I never saw him without his plumber's tools. He was a happy family man now.

The old James, however, was never far from the surface. We were all visiting my mom on a Saturday night in 2003. She was living in a four-bedroom townhouse in Maryland. Tyrell was living with my mom, and he looked fly as always. Tyrell had grown from that delicate boy into a real trip of a young man. He was about eighteen now, and he made his own clothes with a sewing machine—extremely flashy clothes, with ruffles and sashes and shit, the kind I'd never wear. He sold them too, for pretty good money, and he also made money doing clown shows for children's birthday parties. He called himself Woozy, and the kids really loved him. He also made money by stripping for old women! No lie; he had this one group who'd knock on his door every Friday and say, "Tyrell, we're ready!" and he'd go over and put on a strip show for them. His room was all fluffy with colorful cloth everywhere—slipcovers and curtains and shit like that

that he'd made himself. And two little songbirds in a cage. That was Tyrell; he was always a little different.

David was at my mom's too. He had dropped out of high school, which made J.P. really upset. J.P. always thought David could get a scholarship to go to college because he played basketball so well. J.P. even thought David might get a shot at the NBA after college. David, though, he couldn't finish high school. He wasn't acting out or unhappy or anything like that; he just couldn't be bothered. He's the most easygoing motherfucker in the world—happy as a fucking clam. He just don't do shit.

So we're all at my mom's when James tosses a firecracker just as the girlfriend of this neighborhood guy, Danny Boy, happened to be walking by, and she was really freaked out by it. Danny Boy was pissed when she told him, and he came out and started arguing with James. James went off, and I mean *off*. I'd thought he was past that shit. He went after that motherfucker Danny Boy like to tear his head off. My mom was screaming and crying, begging James not to kill him. She'd watched her sons become drug dealers and not one of them dead or in prison, and now that they were out of the life, she didn't want to lose one to a moment of stupid, pointless violence. We finally got James cooled down by reminding him of his babies and his responsibilities and the good life he now had. He finally smiled, but a real smile, not like the cold little smile he used to give before fucking somebody up. "I'll see you tomorrow in church," he said, and I took Nikki and the boys home.

We had a fourth boy now: Marco Marciano. The day after the blow-up with James and the firecracker, I took Nikki and the boys to Virginia Beach and had a good time—the kind of nice, normal family day that I used to see on TV and in the movies but never thought I'd have my own self. We played in the water, ate ice cream, rode the rides on the boardwalk—all of that. We got home to our place in Laurel, and I just got out of the shower when the phone rings. It's Sabrina, and she's out of her mind crying and screaming that they shot James. I'm like, no, James ain't shot. It couldn't be. He's not in that life anymore.

I hauled ass over there to Kenilworth Avenue with my four-five in my fishing box. As I pull up, I see the yellow tape and I know it's true. They'd just taken James away. Sabrina told me he'd run into that same motherfucker Danny Boy, and there'd been words. A rumble erupted, and everyone was fighting. Sabrina was fighting some neighborhood girl, and my brother André got into it with Danny Boy's brother. And James and Danny Boy threw down. Both of them pulled out their guns and opened fire no more than fifteen feet away from each other. James had taken his bullet-proof vest off only minutes before the fight, and he got hit immediately in the stomach. When Sabrina got to him, James was lying on the ground. "I can't believe that bitch-ass nigger shot me," was all James said before he fell out. By the time we got to Prince George's Hospital, James was in surgery. The bullet had gone through his bowels and filled him all up with shit, so he never woke up. To this day I believe if that ambulance had got there earlier, James would still be alive.

I hunted that motherfucker Danny Boy down, and I almost had him. My mom was in the car when I saw the guy coming down the street. Mom was like, Let me go get some cigarettes, and she jumped out of the car. It threw me off just enough that the dude got past me. I think my mom didn't want me killing that guy. It wouldn't have brought James back, and it would have put my ass in prison and left my four boys without a father. The police eventually picked Danny Boy up, but they said James had shot at him first so his killing James was self-defense. They let the motherfucker go. Now he's in prison, but not for killing my brother. I know if the same thing had happened to me, James would have killed Danny Boy and his whole motherfucking family. I think about that sometimes and wonder if I'm not letting James down. But James, he's dead. My boys are alive.

JOHN PRENDERGAST

I'd been searching for ways to create a broader audience for our issues of war and peace in Africa, a way to reach and activate far more people than we human rights activists were capable of. The answer practically fell into my lap. Pure serendipity.

I was invited to attend an event in 2003 in which Angelina Jolie would be speaking about refugees on Capitol Hill. She made a genuine heartfelt speech about the plight of refugees. After the event we had the chance to meet, and it took us only ten minutes to figure out that we should travel to Africa together. She really wanted to go to Congo, and the United Nations wasn't able to take her because of security concerns, so your friendly neighborhood Africa human rights activist was glad to volunteer for the job.

The trip to Congo was very low-key. Angelina was terrific. She slept in small inns, ate refugee camp food, wrote constantly in her journal, spent endless hours with families displaced by the war, and never complained. If anyone had been expecting a Hollywood prima donna, they couldn't have been more wrong. She dressed way down, and not many people recognized her, though every now and then some African kid would yell "Tomb Raider! Tomb Raider!" at her, and she'd flash that million-dollar smile.

We met with Congolese people who had experienced the gamut of human rights crimes that have become hallmarks of what is the world's deadliest conflict since World War II. We listened to gang rape survivors, former child soldiers, and people that had been displaced and re-displaced, as well as raped and re-raped. We talked about the mineral trade that fuels the war, minerals that are used in our cell phones and laptops, connecting us straight to the horrors we were learning about.

When we returned home, the Holocaust Museum offered to host, on its website, a photo exhibit of our trip which featured Angelina reading from her diaries and me talking about the politics of the place. *People* magazine wrote about the website, and so many people clicked on it to hear Angelina speak about the Congo that the Holocaust Museum's server crashed in the first couple hours the exhibit went live. I'm pretty sure it wasn't my political analysis people were logging on to listen to.

The lightbulb started flashing. Hardly anyone's interested—yet—in African wars, but everybody's interested in movie stars. I decided to try to work with some of these more famous folks to encourage them and help them speak out about the people devastated by war so that the survivors wouldn't be forgotten anymore. Most of the celebrities I encountered turned out to be effective and sincere advocates, with an audience full of potential recruits to the cause. These celebrities are the master recruiters, and their impact is huge in terms of raising awareness.

From there, my work with actors, musicians, and athletes began to take shape. I forged a partnership with my dear friend Bonnie Abaunza, who ran the artist relations unit for Amnesty

International; I was again working with one of the groups my high school Spanish teacher Ms. Kane had introduced me to that fateful day at detention when she tossed those pamphlets on my desk. Bonnie and Angelina introduced me to Ryan Gosling, who got very passionate about the child soldier issue in northern Uganda and traveled with me to the internal refugee camps there, where we met many of the kids who had been forced into combat at a young age. Afterward we lobbied Congress, went to the United Nations, wrote articles, and made YouTube videos together. We later went to Congo to make films about the people there and how their lives are affected by war.

I met and talked basketball with Don Cheadle at an early screening of *Hotel Rwanda* arranged by Bonnie and Amnesty. Don and I found that we shared a genuine passion for the antigenocide cause. We ended up traveling to Africa twice together with ABC News, coauthoring two books and a bunch of op-eds, and making speeches all over the country together. The incomparable Samantha Power and David Pressman pulled me into working on Darfur with George Clooney, who is a master tactician

George Clooney and J.P. with the elders from southern Sudan
(photo courtesy of Ann Curry, NBC News)

and serious student of international issues, and with whom I later traveled to Sudan, met with President Obama, and did countless television shows, Congressional meetings, and student events.

You couldn't have found three legislators or diplomats more committed or talented than Ryan, Don, and George. We became great allies and friends, and they made a huge impact in bringing attention to issues of war and peace in Africa.

In 2007, with the backing of a foundation called Humanity United, my longtime friend and ally Gayle Smith and I started an organization called the Enough Project that aims to end genocide and other human rights crimes by continuing to build a political constituency for this cause. As part of the Enough Project, NBA star Tracy McGrady and I traveled with my Darfurian brother Omer Ismail to the refugee camps in Chad, and we created a sister schools program called the Darfur Dream Team that links students in U.S. schools to students in the refugee camps and funds the schools in the camps.

It was right about then—when my dream of getting these issues out to a wider audience was taking shape—that Michael called to tell me James had been killed.

I was in Africa when I got the news, and despite the unearthly heat, I felt cold for days. Precious James, my little brother, a kid who used to be at the Prendergast family reunions down at the shore, was gone, just like that. Talk about *unfair*: James had been right at the point of getting his life together and putting aside the violence that had been his great weakness when a bullet cut him down. I was thankful that he had reconnected with God at the end. I was finding my own way back to my faith, and I found some consolation in that thin silver lining in an otherwise desolate cloud.

mer. He needed to feel the road sliding under him again,
ot in the habit, on my frequent visits, of loading him into
assenger seat of the car and taking him for drives. We had
estinations in mind. I'd try to point the car in a direction
would let the sun stream in on him, which he really loved.
snuggle into a big blanket, talk aimlessly for a while, then
his broad forehead on the window, and close his eyes. The
er had taken a lot out of him, and he had really dodged a
et, but at considerable cost.

On one of those drives, I tried to get Dad to remember the
. In particular, I wanted to know more about the beatings
taken from his father. How often did it happen? Did he
t back? How was he affected by them?

"What are you talking about?" he asked, opening his eyes
lifting his head from window. "That never happened."

I told him Uncle Bud had told me all about it, but Dad just
ok his head.

"No, he got it all wrong," Dad said, wrapping the blanket
re tightly and closing his eyes again. "My dad was the great-
. A good Samaritan, a friend to everybody." He rolled his head
ard the sun and closed his eyes, ending the conversation.

I didn't know what was accurate, given what Uncle Bud had
d me. But between the onset of dementia, the shock of major
ncer surgery, and God knows what kind of psychological scar-
g, Dad may have pushed whatever memories there were of
at side of his father so far down as to be inaccessible. Maybe
e was lucky that way.

I wasn't so lucky, however. Spending all that time with him
ot me reflecting on my childhood legacies. I began to realize
at all the screaming and shaming I had been subjected to in

22. "That Never Happened"

MICHAEL MATTOCKS

I ran into a dude I knew and he told me that my brother Tyrell
had given him a bunch of clothes. Not sold—gave. I didn't
think much of it until this woman friend of ours said Tyrell had
been by to give her his sewing machine. "You mean he sold it to
you?" I asked, and she said, no, he'd given it to her straight out.
Elsie called me that night, and as we're talking, damned if I don't
hear motherfucking birds in the background. "Oh yeah," she
said. "Tyrell gave me his birdies. Aren't they sweet?"

He came by to see my boys, and he was the old Tyrell. Kind
of fly, but sweet as ever. My boys loved him; they'd pile on and
wrestle Uncle Tyrell to the carpet the minute he walked in the
door. The boys and I were planning to go to the amusement
park King's Dominion the next day, and I asked Tyrell if he
wanted to go with us. "Yeah!" the boys all cried. "Uncle Tyrell,
come with us!"

"Okay," he said, laughing, and I felt good.

Next morning as the boys were getting ready to go, I called
Tyrell to remind him. "I'll be there in half an hour," he said. Half
an hour later, the phone rings. It's Elsie screaming her head off.

Tyrell had hung himself.

JOHN PRENDERGAST

The news of Tyrell's death hit me in many ways, but the hardest might have been the wave of concern I felt for Michael. I hadn't spent nearly as much time with Tyrell as I had with James, but I was very worried about how losing a second younger brother might affect Michael. For as long as I'd known him, he'd talked with such laser-like conviction of wanting to protect and care for his family. Now two of his brothers had slipped away, horribly. Michael wasn't able to stop James from being gunned down, and he couldn't stop Tyrell from hanging himself. Michael's lifeboat out of D.C.'s stormy streets, though anchored solidly by Nikki, was relatively new, and he was engaged in a Herculean effort to stay afloat.

I was still going back and forth to Africa, and from my hotel room in Zimbabwe, I spent hours on the phone with Michael, talking through Tyrell's death. (The security agents that usually tapped my phone in Zimbabwe probably felt bad about hounding me that week.) It was a moment I really needed to be Michael's big brother.

Right around the time of Tyrell's suicide, my dad was diagnosed with pancreatic cancer. He had to have major surgery, so the family circled the wagons, and as soon as I got back from Africa, I spent as much time as I could high-tailing it up I-95 from D.C. to Philly to be with him during this critical time.

I had one strangely cathartic incident before Dad was released from the hospital after the surgery. He was hooked up to a lot of tubes, and he would periodically become obsessed with getting up and walking out of that room. Of course he was heavily medicated and needed to stay in bed for some time

before he'd be allowed to move aroun
agitated, and the fairly heavy dosage o
doing the trick. In his half-conscious
ing to pull the intravenous tubes out
get up. I tried to keep his hands away
strain him from rising out of bed. He s
all the old fury of the days of my childh
strange painkiller-induced flashback. He
and threatening me like I was thirteen ag
at first, as I immediately reverted to that
experienced when I was young and scared

But then I remembered an exercise I h
at a workshop given by a famous psycho
imagine yourself as a terrorized little kid in
ful situation from your past, and then you
self entering the picture and protecting that
The exercise that I went through was actual
life. My dad had taken me back to that plac
nerability and fear, but my adult self was abl
the little boy, and tell my dad that what h
what he did all those years—was wrong. I to
him anyway, but he needed to know that it h

Because of the painkillers, I'm not sure he
incident a half-hour after it happened. But a
of peace came over me when things had calme
that I certainly wasn't accustomed to.

Even though he was in a lot of pain, Dad
sitting around the house all day once he wa
the hospital. After all, he'd spent his whole wo
car, driving coolers of Fred's Frozen Foods fr

my youth had left an echoing critical voice burrowed inside my brain, a voice that I simply redirected at myself when my dad wasn't there until it became indistinguishable from my own. The voice would critique and yell and shame me all day long. Sometimes the inner voice would get externalized in sharp, shaming critiques of others. The voice, of course, was quite normal to me, but it was shocking and jarring to those around me. I was just repeating over and over what I had experienced, what I was familiar with. I would often be sharp and hurtful verbally to those around me while thinking I was speaking normally. The result? A hard pushback against any intimacy, including with Jean, from whom I was now separated, a harshness with anyone close to me, and the lead in technical fouls in every basketball league I ever played in.

It was during this time that I finally began to address my own growing depression. My father's illness, my separation from Jean, and the tragically coincidental loss of three close friends all conspired to intensify my omnipresent anxiety. I suddenly perceived a clear choice amidst the emotional wreckage: Either I could construct another emotional wall—my specialization—or I could let the entire edifice of self-protection tumble. I chose the latter route, exhausted from years of ducking and hiding, and the result was difficult but in a small way miraculous. I began to seep. For two months, small tears would trickle from my eyes as I deliberately began clearing the emotional brush inside me, with the help of counseling, reading, and a little prayer.

I spent days and nights going back into my past, finding old friends and family members to interview as I reconstructed parts of my own emotional history that I had completely submerged in my subconscious. The result was painful, but slowly, steadily liberating. I was able to finally draw connections between how I had protected myself as a kid, how I had built more and different walls when I started going to war zones and refugee camps in my early twenties, and how all that fed the ever-present bowling ball of depression in the pit of my stomach.

As a last step in this process, I finally decided it was time to talk to my father about the fraught and explosive subject of our own relationship. After all those awkward dinners out studiously talking about sports, and all the long drives in the sun, I found the courage and the words to ask him why he thought he and I had fallen apart so completely when I was younger.

"You were just completely out of control," he recalled in a hushed but matter-of-fact tone. "You had no direction. Raising hell in the neighborhood, the drinking, the drugs. . . . You needed discipline, J.P. If I was hard on you, it was because it's what I had to do to bring you back in line."

I was so stunned I couldn't speak. Me? Drugs? Drinking? I was first or second, academically, in every school I ever attended. I was an athlete constantly striving to improve. I'd never touched a cigarette or a beer, let alone drugs. I'd been the Lizard! I think I went to one party as a teenager, a painfully alienating experience, and that surely didn't qualify as raising hell in the neighborhood. I never even had a girlfriend back then. I'd spent my teenage years studying, working two or three jobs at any given time, playing basketball, or making music tapes from the radio, alone in the basement. And this is how Dad remembered me? He really didn't know me at all; he had no idea who I was.

Is that how I'd seemed to Michael during all those drug-dealing years? As out of touch with him as my dad was with me?

23. "We See You Out Here All the Time"

MICHAEL MATTOCKS

I keep thinking about that time that Stick called me from jail after stabbing Kenny to death with those barbershop scissors. He was convinced James and Tyrell, who'd watched it happen, had ratted him out to the police. "I hope your brothers die," he told me, and damned if they ain't both dead. It's like he put a curse on them.

Of course, it's me who's responsible. I brought James into the life to protect him, and all I did was get him hooked on the guns and the violence that ultimately killed him. As for Tyrell, I never saw him for who he was—none of us did—and that must have made him so lonely he couldn't take it anymore. I wasn't the only one; I know that. But I was the big brother. It was my responsibility.

So many people that I loved are dead and gone now. Aunt Evelyn, Aunt Frances, Aunt Stella, Uncle Artie, Little Charles, Cool, Cousin Glen who I shot in the leg, Willie, Don, Kenny, James, Tyrell. I loved them all. I had another brother from my dad besides Tyrell and my sister Sabrina, and he's dead too, stabbed to death in prison. His name was Jesse, and he lived with his mother, who died when he was in prison. I hardly knew him, but he was my brother, and without him in this world, a little piece of me is gone as well. Even Shitbag; I miss him too. Man, you live long enough and you end up missing everybody.

I'll tell you what feels good though: I am a real dad in a way no man in my family was ever a dad. We got a fifth boy now: Arturo Giovanni, whom we call Fats, born in 2004. Rolando's a teenager now, tall and slender like his dad. He bucks on me occasionally, but he's a basically a good dude; works hard in school and is nice to his mama and brothers. My four little guys are all stocky like me and just about the happiest little motherfuckers you've ever seen. They have no idea the kind of life I came up in, or the drug dealing that I did. To me, a candy store is a piece of the battlefield; to them, it's a place to buy a treat. I see a homeless shelter and I have to look away, remembering those goddamn Hefty bags of my childhood. But I was down in D.C. with my boys and passed a place where some people were ladling out food to the homeless, and my boys were like, Can we go get some food? They have no idea, living out in the suburbs like we do, what that life was like. That's a good thing. I like it.

What I really love is at night, when Nikki and I are sitting on the bed watching television, and all the boys come in a pile up on us. Those fresh, smiling faces, so relaxed and content. They know a kind of love I never knew. We don't have a lot of money, but that's okay with me. I sleep with both eyes closed. And I'm there for my boys.

They all play football, and Nikki and I go to every practice and every game. Nikki is the team mom. We see very few other parents out there. Last year I was folding up our chairs after a game, and these folks came up to us and introduced themselves; their boy was on the other team.

"We see you out here all the time," they told me. "You're a great dad."

Can you imagine how that made me feel? Growing up with no dad, nobody even to teach me what a dad is? To have some stranger come up and call me a great dad? Man, I'm still floating, just thinking about that.

Front row, from left: Nino, Marco, Arturo. Back row, from left: Lando, Michael Jr., and Michael.

JOHN PRENDERGAST

After surviving the first one, my dad had a subsequent bout with cancer, and this time—in his early eighties—there wasn't much that modern medicine could do. His battle with dementia also was taking its toll on him and on my mom, who grieved for the husband who was disappearing day by day before her eyes. Two nights before he died, Luke and I stayed up all night in Dad's room with him. He was barely conscious, occasionally reaching up for some distant vista that only he was privileged to see, but unable to articulate any of his thoughts. Luke and I talked to him all night, telling him and each other stories of our childhood, choosing to reminisce on the good times, the amazing legacy my father had left. We also told a lot of jokes, and every once in a while Dad would let out a little laugh, so we knew he could hear us.

That night I also had some time alone with him, when Luke went off to spend some time with his family. I was able to tell Dad that although I didn't fully understand everything that had happened between us, I was sorry for what he had gone through with his dad, and I was sorry that we had lost so much time over the years with our battles and my cold silence.

And there was some stuff I wanted to tell him without Luke there in the room. It was then that my tough-guy façade came down. I was able to thank him for doing a lot of good things as a father. I was able to forgive him for the stuff that was bad. I was able to tell him I loved him. And finally, with a lump in my throat, I was able to say goodbye, even though I didn't want him to leave.

My dad's death affected me in all kinds of complicated ways, as you can imagine. But the way that relates most to my long history with Michael is that on the day after losing my dad, I woke with an overwhelming need to find my other little brothers, Khayree and Nasir, whom I felt I had failed spectacularly.

Fifteen years earlier, I'd foisted my responsibility to Khayree and Nasir on Luke, and he kept up with them for years, admirably. But eventually his own family responsibilities led to a loss of contact, and when that happened, I too subconsciously let Khayree and Nasir go. My life had gotten so full, had become so exciting, that it had been all I could do to maintain a shred of brotherhood with Michael and his brothers. Khayree and Nasir had simply fallen off my radar screen.

But never entirely. As soon as Dad died, my desire to find Khayree and make everything right was overpowering. My whole family was gathered at the Berwyn house the day after Dad's death. I excused myself, and then Luke's wife Kim, my godson Dylan, and I drove into the dilapidated old neighborhood in Philadelphia where I used to pick up Khayree and Nasir. We began crisscrossing the streets, looking for a familiar face who might be able tell us where they were. It was futile, stupid, the act of a grief-and-guilt-stricken madman, and it paid off. We came around a corner and standing in the middle of the street like a vision was Khayree's mother, Dicie.

She screamed when she saw us, threw her arms straight up, and praised Jesus loud enough for him to hear it in heaven. Khayree had just gotten out of prison in New York, she said, wrapping me in a hug for the ages, and all he was talking about was finding his big brother J.P. and getting another chance.

"And Nasir?" I asked.

Her face clouded over. "He's dead," she said. "Five years. Shot down on this very street."

She climbed in the car, and we drove to where Khayree was living. I spotted him as we pulled up, sitting on a folding chair in front of a run-down row house, his artificial leg stretched out in front of him. He'd grown much taller, and thicker, in the intervening years, ruggedly handsome and athletic. From across the street, I could see how he slouched over, and I worried whether a lifetime of disappointment and punishment had beaten him down. As his mom and I crossed the street toward him though, his face exploded in a smile, and he struggled to his feet to come hug me. We babbled apologies at each other, and when he asked about my family, I had to tell him my father had just died.

Somehow what seemed right at that moment was for Khayree to just jump in the car and for us to drive straight to the house in Berwyn so we could be a family again and go to my father's funeral together. The house was full of so much sadness that to resurrect Khayree in the flesh, and wash away the pain of his disappearance and the past strain it had caused between Luke and me, seemed exactly the thing to do. As it turned out, walking through the door with Khayree was an important balm for the family, and everyone was really happy to see him again.

For the most part, Dylan and Michael, Luke and Kim's sons, were too young to remember Khayree, and we had to explain to them his importance to the family. The last time Luke had seen Khayree and Nasir, Dylan and Michael were still in their infancy. Khayree and Nasir had showed up at Luke's house for a quick and uncomfortable visit in a brand new car, and they were very cagey about the vehicle's origins. Khayree's reappearance that day, so many years later, certainly couldn't erase all that had happened between all of us, but it was as though some small consolation had been wrested from the sadness of losing my father.

I called Michael in D.C. to give him the news about my father's passing. I could hear his heart break on the other end of the line. He said, "J.P., you know I had no father around. You were my big brother, but Mr. P, he was the closest thing I ever had to a real father."

Well, I suspect a lot of kids felt that way.

Some friend of my dad's wrote an online eulogy after his

death: "I remember Jack being so proud of J.P.'s work in the inner city of Philadelphia." Strange that I never knew that till after he passed away.

The funeral was just as Willy Loman had dreamed. They all came—hundreds of people—with their strange license plates. The driver of our hearse told us he'd rarely seen such a gigantic procession. I stood awestruck at the impact my father had had on so many people. The love ran deep and broad. For years I'd listened to Dad's stories about the road, and I'm sure some small part of me had always suspected at least some of those stories might have been embellished just a little bit. But there they were at the funeral, so many of the characters Dad had been telling stories about for years.

As the older son, it fell to me to deliver the eulogy. I'd stayed up late the night before, and somewhere around two in the morning it struck me —finally—that despite all the tension and misunderstanding, despite the distance I had tried to put between us, I was my father's son. I'd lost sight of it along the way.

The man had given me some endlessly useful gifts. As I told the assembled crowd at St. Monica's Catholic Church, "In all my travels all over the world—in refugee camps, in war zones, in soup kitchens—I have rarely seen such a vibrant combination of giving and loving that my father modeled every day of his life. It is why I am who I am, why I do what I do; and I suspect it is why Luke is a teacher at one of the most challenging schools in the commonwealth of Pennsylvania."

After the funeral, everybody gathered at Jimmy Duffy's restaurant, a favorite place of my father's, to have a few drinks and tell Jack Prendergast stories. Then we took my mother home to the Berwyn house to begin her life as a widow.

We all sat up late that night, and after Mom went to bed, a beautiful thing happened. Luke, Kim, Dylan, Michael, Khayree, and I found ourselves around the dining room table, amid the coffee cups and mourning-cake crumbs, planning out Khayree's life as one big family. Khayree said he wanted to enroll in a school to become a barber, and we Prendergasts challenged each other to help him in one way or another.

The product of several hours of laughing, cajoling, and hard bargaining was a handwritten paper contract that lays out each person's commitment to Khayree's future, including Khayree's own pledges. Rather than enumerate all the ups and downs of that evening's negotiations, I'll just reproduce the document in its entirety. It isn't grammatically correct in all places, but it says everything about Khayree, about the courage and love in my family, and—for better or worse—about the way I take on challenges and then spread them around to make other people share responsibility for them.

July 20, 2008

DYLAN

— challenge Khayree in chess until he beats him twice in a row

— will receive regular haircuts from Khayree

MICHAEL

— will work with Khayree on his essay writing to prepare him for the GED

J.P.

— underwrite GED test and expenses while attending barber school

—pick him up and go to dinners

—help get him placed at a barber shop and be his reference

KIM

—help Khayree find a GED site

—arrange tutoring if necessary for GED

—keep an eye out for Khayree

—pick him up and have him over for dinner

LUKE

—work with Khayree on his essay writing to prepare him for GED

—keep an eye out for Khayree

KHAYREE

—commit to being Dylan's big brother

—take GED within one month

Michael, Khayree, and Dylan

— if pass GED, enroll immediately at barber school
— if fail GED, study and get tutoring and take it again
— finish barber school in a timely manner
— commit to find a job in a barber shop as soon as
you can

We all signed it, and in a typically halting, imperfect way, some of it actually started being implemented, though certainly not all according to plan. Khayree's mom Dicie threw him out of the house because of some infraction, but after he lived temporarily in a halfway house with a group of ex-substance abusers just to have a roof over his head, she eventually relented and let him back in. He was in a car accident that smashed both his pelvis and his prosthetic leg, but he recovered stronger than ever. He became a valued big brother to Dylan, or more accurately they're just brothers, without any big or little attached. They played chess all the time, and occasionally Dylan beat him, but never twice in a row. Khayree studied for the GED, and passed a couple of the test sections. Kim found him a barber who took him on as an apprentice, and she also found him a tutoring program for his GED prep. She and Luke brought Khayree over to their house for dinner on a regular basis.

But suddenly one afternoon, a knock on the door was followed by Khayree's arrest on a dormant parole violation charge. Visiting him in prison and then after his release, we began reconnecting as brothers again. As he overcomes adversity and Team Prendergast expresses our belief in him, he is slowly building self-esteem and a belief that he is capable of more and better. He wants a better life for himself, and he is learning, sometimes painfully, how to overcome the barriers to reentering society after prison, such barriers arising both from his own self-doubt and from the formal and largely unfair restrictions placed on someone with a felony conviction.

If the people running most mentoring organizations were aware that I would finance Khayree's education, I suspect they might not like it. They'd be even less happy that I write Michael a check whenever he needs it. The rap in these programs usually is: Don't help the kids financially because of the perception that becoming some kind of a sugar daddy distorts the relationship. And if the financial help happens when they're young, that perception may be true. But as people try to assume law-abiding adult responsibilities in a world filled with racism, educational disparities, redlining, urban unemployment, and limited opportunities, a little bit of financial help now and then can make all the difference. If Khayree had had a little help at the right moment earlier in his adult life, he might not have done some of the things that set him back so badly.

As for Michael, with five boys of his own, my regular checks are not about making him dependent on me; they're about supporting his very tough choices. He knows that any night of the week he could make thousands of dollars by going back to drug dealing. But he doesn't do it. He stayed with that low-paying job at the hospital, borrowed some money with me as his cosignatory, used it for a course to get a commercial driver's license, got the relevant training while he kept his hospital job and while he totally invested himself in the lives of his precious boys, and then he got a better paying job as a bus driver. He endured the blows to his self-esteem as he remembered how high he rode when he was selling crack, and how he now lives on little because he knows it's the right choice. How can I not want to support that?

It's fine to talk about how relationships should be above money, but if Michael gets in too tough a squeeze, he might feel he has to go back to doing things that could separate him from his wife and boys forever.

I have absolutely no doubt that if the tables were ever turned, he would do the same for me. It may sound like a cliché, but I'm certain we would do pretty much anything for each other now, our bond of brotherhood is that strong.

That brings me to the essence of commitment. The most important lesson I learned while negotiating those peace deals in Africa concerned the difference between passively treating the symptoms of a crisis versus actually committing to addressing the root causes. In a place like Sudan, for example, when the United Nations sends in peacekeeping forces and billions of dollars of food that are critically needed, it certainly saves lives and momentarily treats the symptoms. To resolve the crisis, however, and to keep it from worsening require a far deeper level of political commitment.

As kids, Michael and James were trapped in a series of crises, and for a long time I beat myself up for my lack of commitment to them and to helping them overcome the challenges they were facing. I was reactively trying to manage symptoms of their life-long series of crises, not committing to working with them to really resolve their problems as they might have seen them. I was their big brother, their protector, and by not confronting their reality, I had in some ways betrayed them. I'd been willing to go just so far, and no further. It turned out that yes, Father, he is heavy. So I set him down and didn't carry him for a while.

I went back to the Big Brothers Big Sisters program a few years ago and re-upped. My newest little brother, Jamaar, is tough and guarded, perfecting the art of speaking in monosyllables when he's around me. In earlier years I might've eventually walked away due to the lack of interaction and, ultimately, affirmation. But I'm learning that bonds can be formed that don't have to be expressed verbally, and sometimes just showing up counts for something in the life of a boy whose father chose not to. His grades are way up; he was the valedictorian of his sixth-grade class. He still doesn't say much to me, but he's on the steps ready to go every time I come to pick him up, football in hand, in an apartment on Georgia Avenue just a few blocks away from where Michael and James ruled the streets a little over a decade before. I hope he knows I won't ever leave his side, no matter what might happen, even though that degree of commitment remains unspoken.

Michael and I together have continued to lend an occasional hand to David. Once when he was falsely accused of aiding and abetting a robbery, the court set bail at an unreasonably high

Dylan, J.P., and Michael

amount. Michael called me up late one night with the news, and he said he didn't want David spending one night in that particular jail. So we drove out to Maryland and went to the bail bondsman, plunked the cash down on the counter, and got David the hell out of there. We stayed up with him nearly the whole night at some crummy fast food place, trying to talk some sense into him. I got David a job at a smoothie shop, and he was their prize employee until he got into an unnecessary dispute with one of the managers, after which he was back into the familiar ranks of the unemployed. David is a work in progress, but I continue to hope and suspect that his turning point is coming sooner than anyone might be willing to predict.

My own family is really close now. I visit my mom all the time in Pennsylvania. Either Luke or Mom sits in Dad's seat at the kitchen and dining room tables; I somehow don't feel right sitting there. Even though Mom is pretty self-sufficient, I still can't get used to the idea of someone being married to another for fifty years, and then losing that person and just being expected to move on, eating meals alone at the table you shared for half a century. After a lifetime of running away, suddenly family is everything to me.

A couple years ago I was playing a particularly muscular game of hide-and-seek with four of the Mattocks boys—Lando was off somewhere being a teenager—and as I raced around with Michael's boys, I was flooded with a new sensation. I'd ended up alone. I'd spent my married years traveling too much to Africa—taking the concept of workaholism to a new level—to even consider parenthood. My marriage to Jean didn't last; our separation ended in divorce. Sadly, Jean is one of a number of victims of my single-minded focus on work, though my friendship with her remains a very important part of my life. A small symbol of the end of the marriage came on the day when I had to move our stuff out of the house before it was sold. Jean's things went to her new apartment, but I left most of my belongings right on the curb in front of the house. I sat in my car for hours that afternoon, watching people come by from all over the place to pick through and take what they wanted like seagulls through the Dumpster that had become my personal life.

I used to feel that I'd grow old with no children of my own, but Michael, by his example, is showing me how it can work by doing all the fathering that I haven't yet done. Through his strength, his heart, and his success as a father, he is illuminating a path that I have rejected for years but that I am now thinking about walking myself.

Everyone always says that good things come in threes. I had those three teachers in high school and three role models in San Francisco when I was twenty that laid the groundwork for my devotion to Africa and my little brothers. I took three trips to Africa before I finally found my path, which led me to be a human rights and peace activist.

The best came last. There have been three factors in my redemption, three gifts in the process of dissolving that bowling ball of depression in my stomach and finally reducing the internal storm to a whisper.

The first dose of grace has come from Michael, as I just described, and the light he is shining as an example to me.

The second gift has been my developing spirituality. Stories from the Gospels have particularly spoken to me, such as the Prodigal Son, who leaves the father as a young man full of arrogance and ignorance but finally returns, humbled but wise, asking for forgiveness and reconciliation. In his letter to the Romans, the apostle Paul talks about suffering which produces endurance, which in turn creates character, which finally leaves one with hope that will never disappoint. In that regard, Michael and I are brothers somehow justified by faith.

My faith has deepened and given me a stabilizing and peaceful anchor that my nomadic and restless soul hasn't experienced before. In this arena, I can't discount the fervor with which my mother has prayed for her prodigal son. Like St. Monica's commitment to St. Augustine during his wayward phase, my mom has never let go of my hand over all these years, reminding me with numbing regularity and rock-hard certainty of God's love and forgiveness. My favorite prayer during the services I attend these days is "Lord, I'm not worthy to receive you, but only say the word and I shall be healed." Blows me away every time that such a power exists.

The third gift involves a prison, a woman, and a bolt of emotional lightning. On December 31, 2009, I decided to go visit Khayree during his imprisonment on that horseshit parole violation technicality. My friend Sia, a Yale Law School grad who had decided to spurn the life of a corporate lawyer and defend folks on death row in the Deep South, was in Philly, and I invited her to come with me to see Khayree. It was a scene right out of a Coen Brothers movie, with all of the family members of the prisoners dressed to the nines in their New Year's Eve best while sitting in what must have been one of the filthiest, dingiest waiting rooms in the American penal system.

Sia navigated our way effortlessly and patiently through the bureaucratic maze of visiting regulations, somehow circumventing the immediate family holiday rule, and we were finally inside four hours after we arrived. It was a big room with prisoners and family members all thrown together, with the entire range of human emotion all on display at once.

Finally, Khayree appeared at the door, and I jumped up and we gave each other a hug. He seemed apologetic for his situation, but I was so angry at the system for what had happened that he quickly realized that he didn't need to be sorry for anything to me.

Then the coolest thing happened. I introduced Sia to Khayree, and they started talking. I watched as Khayree began to blossom right before my eyes. Sia's way with him, Socratic and compassionate, brought out his true qualities and his best spirit. As I watched Sia's warmth and tenderness peel back so many layers of Khayree's self-protection, I felt the same thing happening to me. After we hugged Khayree and left the prison, Sia and I went on a drive through memory lane, going around Philly to my old haunts, to the street with the old lady sentinels in South Philly, to the congressman's storefront office in West Philly, and to a church where I used to volunteer in North Philly.

We talked and talked at an all-night diner I had gone to regularly a quarter century before—a really high class New Year's date. As the sun began to come up on the Philly skyline in that humble diner booth, it was a wrap. I had fallen in love. Six months later I was on my knee, shaking and quivering, asking Sia to marry me. In a moment of unrivaled grace and redemption, she said yes.

Sia has given me confidence and the belief that I can stop

compartmentalizing and wearing masks, that I can allow all the strands of my complicated life to be transparently illuminated for another person to see, and that I can be the kind of father and husband I never thought was possible for me. In Congo, my friend Nicole Young had told me something that kept echoing in my head until the night at the diner with Sia: "Find someone who loves you for who you are, not for who they want you to be." In some ways, Sia is for me what Nikki has been for Michael. Nikki has loved Michael for who he is. She didn't ask him to change; he just did.

It took me long enough, but finally my relationship with Michael helped teach me the value of commitment. Now that I've learned some of the most important lessons about being dedicated to someone, I get to live them out with Sia and truly put my heart on the line for the first time in my life. Because of my work and my continuing travel to war zones, I can't help but think of death every hour of every day. Sia, however, fills

J.P. and Sia

me with an eagerness for life that I haven't felt since I was a little kid, when I started building walls against disappointment and judgment and anger, all the things that take away from an open heart.

———————

In the comic books that I loved so much as a kid, as in Greek and Roman mythology, superheroes often make a mess of trying to do good. Screwing up at one point—even hurting somebody they love—is a central part of many of these stories. All we can do is aspire to make it right, and do our damnedest, and hope that things will work out for the better. And they often do. It turns out that all superheroes, even in the comic books, are broken in some way. It is their brokenness, not their perfection, that connects them to a broken world. Their zeal to heal the world is really a reflection of their own inner desire to heal themselves.

On more than a few occasions, Michael has told me point blank that if he hadn't had a big brother investing and believing in him, particularly in those early years, he would have never made the choice to leave the streets behind and that it made the critical difference between his life and those of many of his other friends who weren't able to avoid prison or the cemetery. All those years, Michael had someone who directly or indirectly challenged him to do something with his life, to introduce some measure of accountability where absolutely none existed, to strive for something better. And perhaps that is the best lesson to draw from my long relationship with Michael Mattocks: that any human being, with all our faults and warts, can make a difference in another person's life if we take a risk and make a commitment. No matter how flawed and inconsistent my connection was with him, somehow it was never broken, and that little light may have helped him navigate at times when he needed it most. That's what Michael believes, and looking back, so do I.

24. "You Know You Not About to Do That"

MICHAEL MATTOCKS

I got word the other day that Gomez got fifty-one years for aggravated murder. Gomez! He was just a kid a little older than me when he introduced me to the drug-dealing life. I owe him a lot; he showed me the way into a life that worked for me for a long time. Gomez was a straight-up dude.

But I can't help thinking: There, but for the grace of God, go I. At any time during those ten years I dealt drugs, I could have been shot, killed, paralyzed, or sent to prison for thirty years. Why am I living happily in the suburbs now with my wife and my five sons, instead of dead on the street or in prison?

I like to say that I'm a blessed man, that God watches over me and protects me. But deep down I know that's not the whole answer. Why would God take special care of me—a no-count drug dealer—when any number of young men like me are shot down or locked up every year?

Part of the answer is my mother and my sister Sabrina. Lord knows they've had hard times of their own, but there is a strength in those women, and a steady love that came through even in their darkest hours, that I always knew I could count on.

Part of the answer is J.P. Even when we were the farthest

apart—when I was so deep into the life that I wouldn't go fishing with him, and he was a million miles away in Africa—his love for me, and his confidence in me, kept some part of me straight. A big brother is a powerful thing to have, especially a brother who isn't just part of your family by birth, but who chooses to be, and then lives by that choice—even when it's hard—year after year. I don't know if I would have believed in myself enough to get out of the life, without him believing in me all these years.

What messes with my head, though, is my brother James, who had me, my mom, Sabrina, and J.P. in his life too, but who couldn't escape the streets and his temper even though he was getting his life together. After all the things he survived, James gets killed over a firecracker.

Without Nikki, I'd be in some real shit today. She showed me and told me what I needed to do to be a real man, and she helped me get out of the life. When Nikki met me, she wrote down a vision for what could happen between us. She never stopped believing in that vision, and it all came true.

But when it comes down to it, I've also just had a lot of good luck. Any one of a thousand bullets could have taken me out. Any one of a thousand cops could have put his hand on me and sent me away forever. Maybe God really has decided to keep me safe for my boys.

After all the drugs, guns, and crime, I'm still alive. When I look back on it, while I was still a juvenile, I had already caught three gun charges, two cocaine charges, two marijuana charges, two robbery charges, an assault charge, and a PCP charge. Not one of them motherfucking charges stuck, and I probably had to serve no more than two months in jail all told. God had other plans for me.

I'm no millionaire. This is a different kind of rags-to-riches story, because there is nothing richer than taking care of my family. It's a rags-to-respect story, I guess.

I work a job every day, but being a dad now is what I do. It takes all my energy, and all my time. I like taking my boys fishing over on Chesapeake Bay, or to the amusement park. Sometimes we just stay home and play a game or watch a movie together. What I've found is that there are lots of ways to be a good father; it doesn't have to look like it does on *Leave It To Beaver* or *The Cosby Show*. I am still Michael Mattocks from North Capitol Street and Georgia Avenue. I don't live the stupid, dangerous, illegal life anymore, but I still wear the cornrows. I don't have to deny who I am to be a good father. In fact, I'd argue the opposite is true: That the only way for me to be a good father to my boys is to love them as the man I am.

We were at McDonald's recently—me, Nikki, and all the boys. We were piled up in the minivan going through the drive-through. As I was sitting there waiting for my load of Happy Meals, I realized with a start that I'd been coming to that McDonald's a long, long time. That was the same McDonald's where Cool whipped out his oowop and let fly with a hundred bullets, then hopped in the car and started chewing his burger like it was nothing. And I remembered how much I'd loved that kind of thing back then. I suddenly felt really old, but in a good way. I felt like I'd tasted that dangerous life but then had outgrown it and found a happy and calm place to grow old.

As I was pulling out, this dude walked in front of the van, and I had to bump the brake hard. He looked up and pulled back his shoulders, like, What the fuck you looking at, you bitch motherfucker? I lifted my chin a hair—enough to say, Who the fuck are you? That's all it takes, most of the time, for the guns to come out and the bullets to go every which way. Nikki looked over at me and said, "You know you not about to do that." She'd lost her daddy to a moment like this, and she had no use for me getting us all into a spot. I glanced into my rearview mirror, saw all five of those boys in the back, and looked back at the dude in the driveway. I cracked a grin and nodded my head at the motherfucker, and he softened a little and walked on down the street.

I hit the gas and peeled out of the lot, flinging French fries all over the inside of the van. Nikki was hissing mad. But in the backseat I heard something that made me feel good: One of my boys, whispering to another one in awe:

"My daddy's *thorough.*"

Front row, from left: Arturo, Marco, Michael Jr., and David. Back row, from left: J.P., Nino, Michael, Lando.

Acknowledgments

FROM J.P.

Though I failed at our marriage, Jean played a major role in my life as I slowly matured. Over the years, she has found faith and stability one day at a time, just like me. Though it is hard for her to forget the lost years, she has forgiven me, and we have maintained a bond that defies explanation. I thank her for all she has given me.

My best friend Samantha Power held my hand and never let go during the darkest phases of the last few years, when the weight of accumulated family and war zone traumas threatened my stability. Samantha and I worked together on what we called "the bats in our bat caves," those crippling insecurities and cratering self-doubts that so undermined our ability to be fully ourselves, and to completely love another. We had many an all-night session full of tearful loss, blinding insight, shared fury, and compassionate empathy that more than anything helped us find our way out of our respective bat caves, finally.

From Michael

I want to thank the good Lord for keeping me here and blessing my family. Of all the people in my life, I want to thank my mother-in-law, Miss Sandy (Sandra Jackson), who helps Nikki and me take care of our kids and was always looking out for us, taking us in when we had nowhere to go.

From Both of Us

We thank our precious mothers, without whose prayers and will we wouldn't have made it far enough to write these words. And we appreciate Luke's wife, Kim, who helped find many of the photographs in the book.

Dan Baum helped us write this book. He is the silent third author who skillfully took the huge lump of clay that was our lives, separate and together, and helped us mold it into the beginnings of a real narrative that made sense to us, and more importantly to others. We thank our friend Dan profusely for his dedication to our story, and to us. We also thank our agent Sarah Chalfant, who believed in our story and helped us find a home for this book after six publishing houses turned us down. And we thank our editor, Heather Lazare, who with patience and wisdom further molded the narrative into a real book that we hope will help others learn from our winding but honest journey.

Beyond Reading This Book

Our hope is that more people will realize they can be big brothers, big sisters, mentors, tutors, or whatever. More people will realize they can contribute to making the world a better place, even on something as seemingly far away as protecting human rights in Africa. If you don't have time to volunteer, make a contribution. It all matters.

Here are five organizations we can vouch for:

1. Big Brothers/Big Sisters: www.bbbs.org
2. The Enough Project: www.enoughproject.org
3. Covenant House: www.covenanthouse.org
4. Equal Justice Initiative: www.eji.org
5. Darfur Dream Team Sister Schools Program: www.darfurdreamteam.org

John Prendergast is available for select readings an
about a possible appearance, please contact the Rar
Bureau at rhspeakers@randomhouse.com.

Michael Mattocks is also available upon reques